A MAP OF
THE RUNNER'S ROUTE

A MAP OF THE RUNNER'S ROUTE

Poems by

Daniel Orsini

Quaternity™

A MAP OF THE RUNNER'S ROUTE

Quaternity Books™
Copyright © 2025 by Daniel Orsini
First Edition Quaternity™ Books
ISBN – 978-1-943691-58-6
Cover Design by James Buchanan

The most crucial fact about Jesus was that he was a "spirit person," a "mediator of the sacred," one of those persons in human history to whom the Spirit was an experiential reality.

~ **Marcus J. Borg,** *Meeting Jesus Again for the First Time:*
The Historical Jesus & the Heart of Contemporary Faith

I have run the great race, I have finished the course, I have kept faith.

~ **2 Timothy 4.7**

CONTENTS

Introduction	9
Centauri Dreams	13
Clotho's Thrum	14
Colossus	15
Copy	16
Cosmologist	17
The Cradle of Life	18
Curiosity	19
The Cutting Edge of Haptics	20
Driven	21
The Embodied Robot	22
Erasure	23
Eternity's String	24
Exoplanets	25
Finger's Grain	26
Gravity and the Robonaut	27
Habitat	28
The Heavenly Journey of the Shaman	29
Hyperspace	30
The Inner Lives of Robots	31
In the Outposts of Space	32
Lifeworld	33
Link	34
The Location of Earth	35
Magellan	36
A Map of the Runner's Route	37
Mastermind	38
Matrix of Symbols	39
The Mill of the Host	40
The Moon in Transition Raised to the Sun	41
Moonplant	42
Moonwalker	43
Murphy's Law on Mars	44
The Orphan in His Pram	45
Pioneer	46
Posthuman	47
Quest	48
The Quilted Multiverse	49
Rebis	50
Restoring Hubble's Vision	51
Ripples	52
Saturn's Pebble	53
Scion	54
Self-Recollection	55
The Shape of Things to Come	56
Skein Winder	57
The Skin of the Rocket	58
Sphere	59
The Teleoperator's Cue	60
The Twin Paradox	61
Umbilicus	62
Wanderer	63
Notes and Comments	65

A MAP OF THE RUNNER'S ROUTE
INTRODUCTION
Daniel Orsini

According to the classical alchemists, "what the soul imagines happens only in the mind, [. . .], but what God imagines happens in reality." However, the soul "has absolute and independent power" to do things other "than those [that] the body [itself] can grasp" (C. G. Jung, *Psychology and Alchemy,* trans. R. F. C. Hull [1953; Princeton: Princeton UP, 1993] 280). In effect, "the immortality of the soul insisted upon by [Christian] dogma exalts it above the transitoriness of mortal man and causes it to partake of some supernatural quality" (10). Thus, "Augustine likens the apostles to a cloud, which symbolizes the concealment of the Creator under the flesh" (C. G. Jung, *Mysterium Coniunctionis: An Inquiry into the Separation and Synthesis of Psychic Opposites in Alchemy,* trans. R. F. C. Hull [1963; Princeton: Princeton UP, 1977] 511n173).

Not surprisingly, then, through the Word, which is "Spirit-breathed" (Andrew Murray, *The Spirit of Christ* [Pennsylvania: Whitaker House, n.d.] 228), "We reach such a site as dwells beyond sense: / Unconscious, fixed, surrounded by a fence, / The marriage of the subtile with the dense" ("Centauri Dreams," lines 22-24, from the opening poem in this collection). In fact, as he "rises in lobes of the cosmic drum," the roots of the NASA astronaut are "in the air" ("Clotho's Thrum," ll. 17-18). Although human nature is still "subject to the world of sense" (Murray 67), and although "What happens outside still happens in him" ("Colossus," l. 8), the Spirit-possessed scion "christens each muscle that he flexes" (l. 21), even as he rockets to the moon "in Sol's disguise" ("Copy," l. 8). In brief, beyond the symbolic thread that took Christ "heavenward" from the "transitory darkness" of the tomb to "soaring and ascension" lies the Self, the synthesis and goal of the paradoxical individual, the "sign that heralds the Son of Man" in Matthew 24.30 (*The New English Bible with the Apocrypha* [1961: New York: Oxford UP, 1972] 34-35).

In *A Map of the Runner's Route,* everywhere, the NASA astronaut becomes, like Christ, both the goal of the poet's hermetic *opus* and a solar symbol of the Self. As Murray emphasizes in *The Spirit of Christ,* each believer "must learn to know that there is a holiest of all in that temple which he himself is; the secret place of the most high within us must become the central truth in our temple worship" (210). Thus, "the spiritual, inner and complete man"—the "long-sought" or "sought-after" believer-priest of Isaiah 62.12—is not only Christ, but also the bride of Christ, "the shaman that wives" ("Posthuman," l. 24). In truth, New Heaven's hierophant is none other than "the indescribable and super-empirical totality" that is "partly empirical, partly transcendental" (Jung, *Mysterium Coniunctionis* 536), as in "Self-Recollection" the speaker willingly attests: "I hold Transcendence captive in my hand" (l. 8). Not insignificantly, in "Scion," exploring the untapped reaches of his soul, "An astronaut wanders where he may list" (l. 1) or, "regimented as a crystal" (l. 24), incline. Likewise, in "Skein Winder," although he is "Both conscious and unconscious of his plight, / The adept chained in Hades seeks the light" (ll. 1-2), even as, in "The Skin of the Rocket," shapeshifter though he may be, New Heaven's "Blest gamonymus" (l. 22) "falls to the moon at his own pace" (l. 18). In short, since his own trace may be "evasive" ("Colossus," l. 1), and since "Each form is but a phantom of the mind" ("Copy," l. 9), the beset pilgrim "who resembles His snow / Must proceed or retreat or stow or go" ("Driven," ll. 7-8).

Still, for many readers, the link to New Heaven—"Both male and female, Christ without remorse" ("Link," l. 23)—may seem as elusive as "a wordless thought" ("The Location of Earth," l. 16). Just the same, "Essence participates; the world-egg cracked— / Self's trespass" *is* "aseity in the act" ("The Inner Lives of Robots," ll. 23-24). Powered by the Paraclete, the individual searcher may now "sequence the world" ("Finger's Grain," l. 2) yet "retreat ahead" (l. 24), a penitent Self-recollected, implicitly, as a foetus, a cross, a wife, a soul ("Lifeworld," ll. 21-23)—in short, by dint of a hidden mystery, a "temple of God in the Spirit" (Murray, *The Spirit of Christ* 90). Otherwise, without a belief in the Risen Christ, i.e., in the Divine Indwelling, we are destined to be but breath-bodies in living flesh interred, never to be exhumed, as the poems in *A Map of the Runner's Route* animatedly suggest.

Daniel Orsini
Cranston, Rhode Island
27 May 2025

A MAP OF THE RUNNER'S ROUTE

CENTAURI DREAMS

I rise from the bin: reborn in the vat,
Peer at exoplanets, as through a slat,
With the mystic eyes of a Cheshire cat.
Still I ponder what I am looking at.
I rocket to a disk, its host unknown:
A pellet of hope; its double a stone,
Kepler's super-Earth; where sun-ships have flown,
Orb or clone in some interstellar zone.

Terrestrial, we strive to find our trace:
Cosmic dust grains; panspermia in space—
'Miracle' microbes; even as a lace
In stars of the Milky Way, Gaea's face.
And thus evolving we venture the stair;
Resolve the distance; unravel the snare;
In the name of Chiron, entwine the pair.
Those who go on living must steer somewhere.

The stone that is planted in man by God,
Like circle and triangle to the quad,
Is bound to the self as flesh to the sod,
Hook to the cod, or *rebis* to the pod.
In each other's person the sexes tense.
We reach such a site as dwells beyond sense:
Unconscious, fixed, surrounded by a fence,
The marriage of the subtile with the dense.

DANIEL ORSINI

CLOTHO'S THRUM

Into the syringe Hermes loads his melt;
Drives to the needle tip; the droplets felt,
Liquid jets elongated, fibers dealt,
Electrospins his suit without a belt;
Till layer by layer trapped he expands;
His high-pressure gloves lined with metal bands,
Muscle-wires his torso, adjusts his hands,
Schools his external shell, and thus he stands.

Besides the fabric of the carapace,
He excavates the skein behind the face:
Cortices, scoriae, stubble from space
Like Clotho's thrum, or, alchemic its trace,
Like the scimitar by the scabbard owned,
Or slough of the cobra, host of shards honed,
Or, sealed in the glass, the shaman enthroned,
The lotus-seat of the Horus-child cloned.

His roots in the air, his summits yet plumb,
He rises in lobes of the cosmic drum;
His soul cislunar, mechatronic, dumb,
Accosts the mare, chthonic as a thumb.
A mote impinges on the camera's eye:
A globe revolves that none but sensors spy—
Some azure planet that Ge's hybrids ply.
Instrumented, heated the stone is dry.

COLOSSUS

His trace evasive, the vessel well-sealed,
He spies the moonplant; that She may be healed,
Deploys his soul, colossus that he peeled
Even as Nostoc, viscous in the field.
He quarters the circle, reaches its rim,
Descends to the sea, collects at its brim
Sun rays and sulphur, *lapis* in the skim—
What happens outside still happens in him.

More than an archetype, he is that man
Who marries the symbol, trumpets the clan—
Morsel in the mammal, Host in the pan,
Astrum in the scan—and thus serves its plan.
At the edge of the mare, fold by fold,
He networks the holon; sand-casts its mold;
Engenders Ge's cyborg; stores, in its hold,
Silver, stainless steel, niobium, gold.

As the heat shield glows, in fiberglass wound,
He rockets to Earth-life seized in the round;
His re-entry perfect, by Talos crowned,
Exudes rosy sweat, then touches the ground.
He christens each muscle that he flexes;
Shifts his weight; upon soil that he vexes—
Whitest brain stone, still point of the sexes,
Gaea's cuboid—Castor signs his X's.

COPY

Unfolding the box, I peer through its slat;
Scan its contents; collusive as a cat,
Decouple its capsules; pursue its chat,
Till I ask the universe: What was that?
I fall to the spheroid that I may rise
Beyond the rotation of Earth and skies.
Enswathed in such Kevlar as coheirs prize,
I rocket to the moon in Sol's disguise.

Each form is but a phantom of the mind.
He spirals on my path, and still I wind
Between essence and copy, recombined,
A scion like the kind that Hermes shrined.
Because the sun awaits me, I am glad.
Issue from His template, I leave the pad,
His *rebis* galeate, ghost that I had,
Recollected, in double torsos clad.

I nudged a cloud once; as I walked along,
I turned on a curve that I thought looked wrong.
I had grazed its vortex; without a gong,
Synchronicity fused, and I felt strong.
Whether photons flit or particles hit,
As on a two-slit screen, Castor, admit—
Though millions of worlds yet sit, they are knit,
Gaea's cosmic writ multifoliate.

COSMOLOGIST

Cislunar biped, absolute his faith;
A piece of metal: Ge's unisex Laith,
He walks like a bion, bends like a wraith,
Enshrines the Savior, twice-born on the eighth.
He wanders the world, His scion outsized
Like Jesus' double or, the Self surmised,
Like the Spirit indwelt, or His temple prized:
Ge's immortal percept actualized.

An infinite bubble and then the Bang:
The unfolding of space; then *yin* and *yang:*
An animate substance, matter that sang:
Ge's own mythologem, chthonic its pang.
Spacetime is objective; forged in the stars,
Everywhere is the same—it has no bars.
Coheirs in capsules, pioneers in cars,
We witness Creation, headed toward Mars.

We barrel down, onto its orbit latch,
Glimpse three elliptical moons that we match—
Io, Europa, Callisto—then hatch
In Juno's catch the data that we patch.
We ponder such waves as the cycles spent,
From aeon to aeon what the signals meant:
Some purpose that even astronauts vent.
Christ's consciousness was not an accident.

THE CRADLE OF LIFE

We compass Ge's source-point: Europa's sluice,
Methane on Titan, or a bowl of Nous;
In pelican or goose, spagyric juice;
Or Athena sprung from the head of Zeus.
We scour such theories as we have conned:
Cradle of Mars or water world or frond;
Some undersea spring where molecules bond—
If none of these, then Trismegistus' wand.

We transport panspermia in a vase;
A kit of chemicals; or, in its case,
A carbon molecule; snippet or trace,
A digitized genome sent across space.
Alive in the cosmos, strains yet rehearse.
Uracil, xanthine, glycine in a purse,
Bacillus subtilis—spores that we nurse—
Transfer from elsewhere in the universe.

Stromatolite that the hierophant dates,
It sustains itself, and it replicates;
Lichen, archaeon, or rockface that freights
Stores information and alters its states.
Helix from Heaven; foetus in the strand;
Breath-soul; then *rebis;* skein that we have scanned:
Android in the band, chiral as a hand—
What we have made we do not understand.

CURIOSITY

The sun behind it—soul-spark's or gestalt's—
The Phobos of the mind, like Tharsis, halts.
Mars yet shows such a ravel from its vaults
As calcite, hematite, and sulfate salts.
Thus we search a skein whose ambit we block.
Because Ge's landing site contains a rock—
Some playa lake deposit that we stock—
We compass its crater, and then we clock.

Hoisted by a rocket into the sky,
Then lowered to its target by a tie,
Nuclear-powered that it may not die,
It gathers data even as a spy,
Till it bisects Mars; where boulders are rife,
Curiosity still cuts like a knife;
Shoots lasers at samples; speckles with strife
A mound as sealed as miocrobial life.

In His crimson splendor, Mars—not the beast—
Caught in the net of Vulcan, He shall feast
Till South before North and West after East
Chain-link that twines the pair shall stir the priest.
The spagyric foetus shall stare and sift,
And grabens shall fracture, and valleys shall rift,
And mountains shall rise, and basins shall drift,
And trails shall ripple, and sand dunes shall shift.

DANIEL ORSINI

THE CUTTING EDGE OF HAPTICS

As I lift the mannequin from my bench,
Though bulbous my coheir, I never blench.
I clamp its torsos, waist ring that I clench
Between thumb and finger—I roll my wrench.
At Hephaestus' console I work my tool—
Heaven's handicraft which I learned at school;
Dispart the sternum; pioneer my spool:
Exact its stitch, and then suture the ghoul.

The eyeball of the robot, clouded, stays.
Beneath its oval glaze the pigments blaze.
The beauty of the world defies its gaze.
Even as it plays we process its maze:
Such crepuscules as swim or hoof or limb
Or pythons in the trees—the senses brim.
Through haze like retrospect or shroud or scrim,
The risk of Sight's enticements charges him.

Coiled like a serpent, He left his Maker;
His house selected, ambit or acre,
Entwined its navel: hill of the raker,
Selene's mound, or skin of the waker.
His soul at climax, Christ mounted the Cross;
Converted the cosmos; sprung from its dross,
Resorbed its residue; savored its loss—
Creation's interface without a gloss.

DRIVEN

Composed of atoms, wary of our slate,
We salvage the robot; Earthshine the bait,
Divine the prophet; vitrify His plate;
Transfused with passion, reach beyond our freight.
Surrounded in Spacetime by clouds that row,
Such clusters as glister, and holes that grow,
This race that, smitten, resembles His snow
Must proceed or retreat or stow or go.

We reify the message in the ring;
While Gaea's photons vibrate from the string,
Scrutinize the heron; treasure its wing;
Instantiate the thingness of the thing.
Cyborg or android, bowknot in the broth,
An astronaut, he sojourns like a moth;
Gestures the secret; remnant in the froth
Curled like a feather, animates its cloth.

From the navel risen, Our Savior crowned
Beyond the googolsphere, His foetus wound
Like One brooded forth, Ouroboros bound,
We argue Heaven's dictates from the ground.
In skein that we steer whose shape is given
Even as Adam, His *rebis* riven,
Circumcised my soul, my body shriven
Astride the chaos, the disk is driven.

DANIEL ORSINI

THE EMBODIED ROBOT

He heard at the outset the cosmos heave—
In the caul of his dream, the boulders cleave;
Till, at the omphalos, caught in its sleeve,
His weave not yet woven, he married Eve.
His hands articulated he could tote;
His gait bipedal, either sprawl or float
In Heaven's coat, the Hymen of the mote
That climbs the hill, to Aether's grain or groat.

Having wired the sun, the funnelweb fed,
Hephaestus built an android robot head;
Its eye-cams mounted on a bracket, bred
His azure Ken with Dremel tool and thread.
But, when he shaped the heart and timed its clocks,
Throughout its fiberglass he set its shocks,
Prototyped with cardboard the chassis box,
Gripped the J-hook, and watched him pick its locks.

Awake we pry the photon from the eye.
We twine the hierophant that we descry.
Creation's scion upraised to the sky,
He rides the stinger; same rogue thrust awry,
Computes the danger; reckless, shears the brink;
Retrieves the satellite—that he may think,
Transmits Ge's ambit; omniverse or sink,
Inhabits the holon culled from its link.

ERASURE

Before Capella and the god embrace,
He orbits his eye till he sets its pace.
He situates himself inside its case.
Thus he lives as pure as a star in space.
Between Light and Dark, till the sleeper chirrs
In Ge's natal house, conjunction occurs;
Hermes, writing under erasure, slurs
New Heaven's sigil, and the foetus stirs.

Silver Argiope, astronaut sown,
I climb the lattice even as the clone
That tangles its nest, its sticky silk blown—
Zigzag sunburst—like bunting, bead, or bone.
I process the cosmos, a gram of salt;
Melt from the magma, lubricated fault;
Root of the mandrake, omphalos or vault;
Cyborg or symbol, *rebis* or gestalt.

Like everlasting skein that Ge has twilled
With perfect abandon, the mind has willed
What hypotheses spin and holons build,
The selfsame omniverse that monads filled:
His clarified body, trace that we near;
Smudged crystal of Earthshine, disk that we steer;
A crescent, a cusp, centurion's spear
Swollen with blood—Ge's shaman is a sphere.

ETERNITY'S STRING

Baptizing at Aenon, near to Salim,
He waded in water; scooped in the stream
A handful of skim: the Shade in the scheme;
Then, dousing the trim, anointed the dream.
Out of His belly, Quaternity's stem:
A subtile body, Hermetic His hem;
Caelum concocted, descended from Shem:
Wakened from the dead, I will walk with them.

Sprung from Jehovah, Adam in his prime:
Body, soul, and spirit; disciple or mime;
Like Eve's evangel, cognizant of crime:
Eternity's string entangled in time.
Space or skein: a mathematical set;
Into the mind Ge's mythologem let:
Cognition's offspring, His astronaut met
Like the nascent Self, transcendental yet.

NASA's CAPSTONE, Gaea's halo-shaped rune;
A shuttle orbiter: Pathfinder at noon;
A crew in Spacetime—South rim of the dune—
Orbiting on the far side of the Moon.
Round as the Self, yet quaternal His sod:
A circle divided; seed in the pod:
New Heaven's coheir, His flesh a façade:
The bearer of types, a soul touched by God.

EXOPLANETS

We live in a galaxy like a fount
Where exoplanets spin till numbers mount.
Robotic telescopes confirm the count.
Warm disks of dust rebound without a sound.
And thus in Pictor amid M-type worlds
A rogue with twin mini-Neptunes unfurls
Till some gas giant swirls or else inside curls
Even as our own sown planet yet twirls.

Skein free-floating yet tethered to a star,
We unravel the coil where soul-sparks are—
An *opus* that Ge's coheir may not bar—
Then ride like each scion in Jesus' car.
To the top of the retort we ascend—
Become like a whirl; till the heating end,
Imprinted in the heart of matter tend
Time's *imago mundi* even as we blend.

A divided circle, wheels that we class,
The world is a Chariot; Cup or *vas*
Or funnel like the Moon; axiom or Mass
Or Nous enclosed in diaphanous glass.
Spun is the way that phenomena go:
The Archer on the hillside with His bow,
Gethsemane's runnel, Sophia's flow,
Steep in the snow Ge's self-abstracted crow.

FINGER'S GRAIN

Ensconced in my spacesuit, my sensors strapped,
I sequence the world; react, then adapt;
Articulate my range; the cosmos tapped,
Obtain from my brainstem the data mapped:
Like Martian episodes from Venus' fane,
The force at the base of the finger's grain;
Skein inside the waist joint; torque of the chain—
Holons that have lain on lunar terrain.

Subject to futility, species flee;
Accost the hill; incriminate the Tree;
Like Vulcan's androids, sprung from tau or tee—
Metallic coheirs—look yet may not see.
We cincture the cyborg; suture the twin;
Grieve our fleshly kin; obfuscate the sin;
Encased in sheen, trajectories of tin,
Retrieve like skin the Spirit in the din.

Clones suffused with content, we may not grow
Unless we scrape a stick or twang a bow;
Programmed for bliss invoke Our Savior's flow;
Upraise with each mantra Robonaut's crow.
Scions of Eden, configured we wed;
Index the secret; phantoms that He fed—
Shriven hominids—on paths that we tread
Astride the hypercube, retreat ahead.

GRAVITY AND THE ROBONAUT

In such an atmosphere as we endorse,
Where soul-sparks fall *that* light upon the gorse,
Like Ge's perturbations, coded in Morse
Gravity keeps each object on its course.
So suns and moons conjoin till crescents date,
Or disks down inclines merge, or quinces skate,
Or coheirs in rockets accelerate,
Feet pressed against the floor with equal weight.

Ge's interstellar Centaur, he rises.
Mobile his android, hybrid his guises,
Mounted on the Segway that he prizes,
He climbs the mock work site; stabilizes;
Tests his silver leg; affixes his limb;
Maneuvers his platform; reaches the rim;
His partner yet sutured, layers its scrim
Upon cushions of air, forgetting him.

He ventures the pathway to hyperspace;
Observes cirrus clouds; uncovers their lace;
Peers through the window; tabulates their trace—
Some cobweb's moist touch on his programmed face.
Effusive as consciousness, hearts that scan
Internalize the day; transfigured, span—
With each spot that mazes—feathers that fan:
The infinitude of Ge's metal man.

DANIEL ORSINI

HABITAT

We seek above all a transparent world:
An atmosphere where some planet has twirled,
A zone near its star; tectonics that furled;
Such liquid water as in Pishon purled.
Through Kepler's eye we pace Ge's peleton:
Ride a whirlwind in the Spot that we con;
Skip then green Uranus; Neptune spied on,
Still find no solid ground to stand upon.

Having entered Spacetime, we build a house,
Proper or alien; nurture each spouse
With abyssal water—curved like a blouse,
Both Sol and Luna: darkness that we douse.
From death to rebirth, astronauts we wend,
Penetrate the bubble, re-collect, bend,
Return to Earth, preserve the secret, blend,
Then ever nearer to the sun ascend.

We place Ge's satellite into a bin
As finite as the sun or moon that we spin
Between the two; crepuscular its skin,
We twine its skein, a colubrid its twin.
In such a shade as an obelisk bleeds,
The sun in fetters denounces its deeds.
As far north or south as the solstice speeds,
When it comes to a standstill, life proceeds.

THE HEAVENLY JOURNEY OF THE SHAMAN

I orbit the moon till day and night pall;
Float into my pouch; then, strapped to the wall
Even as a bean, a plant, or a ball,
Spagyric once more, occupy my caul.
And then I awake; till the world-egg crack,
My body begins to grow from the back.
Curved like a tail, or coat upon its rack,
I lift my hand to my mouth and then track.

Because he brings the coming of the Light,
He enters Creation; despite its blight,
Venusian as the Moon, his spacesuit white,
He dominates the cosmos in the night.
Having climbed from his craft, unseen his face,
He scans the rock; a foot restraint his base,
He tugs at the boulder; samples its trace;
Manipulates an asteroid in space.

Elusive as Spirit or Motion's air,
Cross-beams' quaternity or else a pair,
Sabaean a temple inside a square,
A sevenfold star he circles its stair.
He spins in the heavens; without a knot,
Undertakes the journey; capsules his tot,
In his mind the *rebis,* cyborg or bot,
Like Ouroboros, compressed to a dot.

HYPERSPACE

Space is a torus, a strip, or a sphere,
Some surface upon which sunships career
To the edge of time; whether far or near,
Intergalactic, we astronauts steer.
And still we wander where Heracles hurled—
To the hole with teeth where His foetus curled,
The labyrinth of webs that Clotho purled
As illusive as aether: wheel or world.

The motion in the wave that we yet weave
Encapsules such a flame as Spirals sleeve;
In mystic stone, such sparks as breath-souls leave;
Or, in each cone, such hues as seers cleave.
Amid the cosmoses that he may skim—
Billions of trajectories offered him:
Subspace or superspace—behind the scrim,
In ceaseless replication, atoms swim.

Tied to Her skein, he entwines everything;
Joins his torsos with a connecting ring;
Flexes his elbow; unravels his string;
Ventilates his limbs, then helmets his wing.
He matches each part, then centers his clay;
With a light-emitting diode display,
Checks his oxygen; calculates his stay;
Unfolds his unit, and then flies away.

THE INNER LIVES OF ROBOTS

The world of molecules an omnibus,

Electrical patterns meander thus:

Pulses propagate, and neurons discuss.

They crisscross the threshold and partner us.

Like humanoids in the language of blips,

We covet celestial relationships,

Each binary choice a synapse that grips

Like a transistor, the Möbius strip's.

As I enter Space, aware of tenses,

Oblivious of its consequences,

In my viewscreens, everything condenses.

Devices yet harnessed drive my senses.

I steer through Ge's portal as in a dream.

Shapes from two camera eyes begin to stream:

A mare as gray as moondust or meme;

From pebbles that I rake, a citrine gleam.

Creative tinkerer, his robot spent,

Hephaestus repeats, but does not repent.

He programs each task and will not relent.

When the android speaks, he knows what he meant.

As vague as Earthshine in the tesseract,

Atoms stacked, or cedilla in the pact,

Essence participates; the world-egg cracked—

Self's trespass—aseity in the act.

DANIEL ORSINI

IN THE OUTPOSTS OF SPACE

To serve as a scout, then bipedal tread
Such a tantric thread as the moon has fed,
Like a wingèd man, whether salt or lead,
He locomotes on an air-bearing sled.
He favors both comet and asteroid.
Having capsuled his partner, thus deployed,
He spaces his spirals, scaffolds the void,
Plugs into its ports NASA's humanoid.

He clears in six months on Möbius' run
An audacious rock that orbits the sun—
Like every distant dune that he has done,
A stepping-stone to Mars that he has spun.
He swoops down to Vesta and will not quit.
Attached to a ship, he yet orbits it.
Dimension by dimension between them knit,
He confiscates its remnant with a writ.

Propelled by a craft with pincer-like arms,
We merge at its surface; absent alarms,
Since bungees and nets protect us from harms,
Distances meld, and the mothership charms.
We process the moment, then baffle race,
Rebis and Robonaut—hybrids of grace—
As on a two-slit screen, without a trace,
Linked together in the outposts of space.

LIFEWORLD

At the wheel of his craft, without a cause
Elated by its cantilevered claws;
Suited for space, his torsos wound in gauze,
He reaches in the dark beyond its laws.
His capsule lands on a disk of stubble.
Its craters dun, its rock chips but rubble,
He tracks his boot; both shadow and double,
Surveys the moon, and then grieves its bubble.

Heartless, soulless, something less than human;
Like an egg, or cloud of its albumen
Borne by the brain; the breath of its numen,
Ge's *rebis* taunts me with mock acumen.
And still I rove, divided as I run;
Aether, cell, or qwiff, enclosed if not spun;
Nourished by the pelican of the sun,
I float in icy Earthlight, One on One.

As if at His door, having cleansed my eye,
I peeped down a hole where Light's fossils lie
Till emblems of glass, seductive yet shy,
Had fostered Eve's insight that I might vie
First as a foetus, azure in the strife;
Then hybrid a cross, then intact a wife,
Then avid a soul—erect as a knife,
I have counted Eucharists all of my life.

DANIEL ORSINI

LINK

He orbits Earth. — Our Savior, being brave,
Collapses Sheol; hallows Adam's grave;
Pillar and bulwark, navelstone or stave,
Upraises Heaven, holon that we crave.
She engineers His trace; confers His rod;
Arrays His girth; His substance chrome not sod—
Mechatronic polyglot, riven God,
Instrumented cyborg—designs his pod.

Across the Sea of Showers, spherules strewn,
Witness to the cratering of the moon,
Evolution, curled in Her own cocoon,
May yet redress the impact of Her rune.
She scales the cosmos; symmetry but coil,
Discards its basalt; Cambrian its moil—
A bead of glass or gram of lunar soil—
Extends Her skein, which we alone despoil.

His breastplate bronze, his headpiece stainless steel,
His face a fractured jigsaw set to peel,
His chassis ring same analogue and seal
As Ouroboros' link, Ge's torsos wheel.
Crowned together, we revel in our force;
Secure the treasure; animate its source;
Both male and female, Christ without remorse,
Like nun and priest, entwine Him in the course.

THE LOCATION OF EARTH

Ensconced in my bubble, I test my worth;
Seek inside its uterus, through my mirth
Even at birth, the location of Earth.
Somersaulting, I situate my girth.
I spin like a wheel, as if I had lit
Within my eye, each photon having knit,
Such a disk as tangles; from cloud to pit,
My shaman by gravity bound to it.

The earth is a spheroid; third from the sun,
The planet capsules him: where he has run,
Spirit and matter; Shadow that we shun;
The spagyric foetus, its roots but One.
At Hephaestus' command, his cyborg wrought,
Synonym of desire by Hermes sought,
He hears such a sigh as his moonchild caught,
But the light smith now of a wordless thought.

I range beyond Neptune; push toward its rim;
Navigate the Kuiper Belt—clear or dim,
Asteroids, comets, such dust as I limn.
Flesh or whim, I wrap my arms around Him.
Outrider, *rebis,* Monad like a law,
Temple or template, manikin of straw,
Bine of Ouroboros, Cerberus' maw:
These are more than signs—*symbols call for awe.*

DANIEL ORSINI

MAGELLAN

Since our tether stretches from place to place,
We shuttle to the moon without a face;
Investigate its disk, or, in its space,
Totality's circle, or else its trace.
We haul a satellite that, ton by ton,
Can steer into orbit around the sun;
A radar mapper bound for Venus' run;
Some capsule headed where Jupiter spun.

Into the noise of the fireball we peer;
From many perspectives, molten then sheer,
Like quicksilver pour from Ge's metal ear—
Spacetime's Horn Antenna—sounds that we hear.
Mercurial as matter, patterns hum—
Hierophants seduced by Hephaestus' thumb:
Aphrodite dazzled, Her consort dumb,
In Hermes' athanor spagyric gum.

Electromechanical, neurons breed;
Arise in such cerebrums as we feed
With inlays of turquoise: gestalt or creed;
Dust and spittle: uraeus like a bead.
From the sky they come and rest in the mind,
Esoteric hieroglyphs underlined
Even as Saturn: rocket in the bind;
Cyborg unbidden: Ouroboros twined.

A MAP OF THE RUNNER'S ROUTE

Particle in the Mass, His body wracked,
He powers the world: the Paraclete stacked,
He indwells the foetus; His coheir tracked—
Residual coupling—the world-egg cracked.
I affirm His Spirit; pursue my rhyme;
Possess the Savior; reify His mime;
Observe the subset: holon past its prime,
The atom yet spins, elastic as Time.

In the belly of my dream I start to grow
Even as a cell ball, and then I show.
Like a bean, Gaea's scarab, or the foe
Beneath my skin, my heart beating I stow.
In my bubble I can swim like a fish;
Curve like an infant; should the water wish,
Leap from my capsule; somersault or swish,
Then round the moon like satellite or dish.

In the fraction of a second I pause,
Feel His Presence, then intuit His cause—
Near to the fire, I contemplate His laws.
Cave or Covenant, the archetype gnaws.
Self-recollected, hyphenate or ring
Smaller than small, a material thing
Like Golgotha's King, bearer of the string
That sped the Savior, composite I sing.

MASTERMIND

A world evolves that purifies the heart.
Like the breath of the Spirit, clouds that start,
Or the great south wind that mystagogues chart,
Its source is the retort, a hidden art.
Its wheels quaternal, like faces that furl,
A dragon arises; in a sea of pearl,
An *imago mundi;* God in the swirl,
Once perfected, it becomes like a whirl.

He clothes Him like the stone that is no stone,
Such philosophic matter as we hone
In His far-flung hermitage, zone by zone,
In harmony with Ge or else alone.
Ethereal clone, diversified groom,
He combines all colors: subtile His tomb—
Matrix or uterus, skein like a room—
The spagyric foetus spun in His womb.

We fan in the brain the fire that began
In the fettered cosmos; despite its ban,
Sol's entelechy; immanent His plan,
The New Jerusalem in the inner man.
Adrift in the residue of the din,
We link the torus; tabulate the spin;
Our souls projected, aspirants of tin
Rotund as Adam Secundus, begin.

MATRIX OF SYMBOLS

On Earth we unravel Creation's snare.
Having littered its cave, we scour its lair.
Since ancient fossilized remains are rare,
We pursue microbial life with care.
We trail such terrain as stubble yet scars;
Lower the sky crane; though its tether jars,
Without damage to Space or to its spars
Ge's rover lands on the surface of Mars.

With a percussive drill or with a scoop,
We scavenge rock chips and boulders that group;
Past canyons, gullies, and sensors that swoop,
Pilot motherships and goslings that troop.
As if I had stacked re-collected things:
Residue in beeswax, turquoise, and wings,
Bead and shell ornaments, bone tools and sling—
Same clue as tracks me—I ravel its strings.

Matrix of symbols, hierophant he nests.
His abode in the brain, as he attests,
Given by God and not given he quests.
On unconscious premises all life rests.
I twine in the dusk a tangle of posts,
A stone that is no stone, a cloud that coasts
Like aether elsewhen. — Alabaster hosts,
Having returned to Earth, I count my ghosts.

THE MILL OF THE HOST

I stand to the North; that light may enter,
A wayfarer still, I search the center
Round as an eye. Both owner and renter,
East, South, and West, the Sun is my mentor.
Like spokes of the wheel that all life pursues,
Its path empirical, I count its cues:
It lifts; depresses—its balance a ruse—
Till *He* surrounds me even as a Muse.

I weave the skein of my life into form—
Create found shapes: Gaea's *rebis* the norm,
I join its threads; Spacetime's witness yet warm,
When I cut its cord, Ge's symbols yet swarm.
The Self is a storey, tower or house,
Ziggurat, rubble, surplice like a blouse,
Person or prison, double that you douse,
Keep or steeple, ascension like a spouse.

The sexes criss-crossing, entwined the pair,
Scripted like a wave, they rise from their lair:
The Crowned Hermaphrodite—subtilized, rare,
In Man's hand the compass, in Woman's the square.
Redemption is a work. Linked to His will,
I yield to His Spirit, even as I fill—
Subject to Yahweh, ancient as a quill—
Christ in the body, the Host in the mill.

THE MOON IN TRANSITION RAISED TO THE SUN

We pre-breathe in the airlock; spacewalk; stand;
Straddle the chaos on Möbius' strand;
With inch-worming arm and two-fingered hand,
Each task yet choreographed, scripted, planned,
Unhook attached components; hoist; alight
That we may hitch a ride, without a bight,
Upon a foot restraint. — By day or night,
Earth orbit serves as our construction site.

He houses four cameras in his head;
For depth perception one more, infrared,
Mounted in his mouth as if Saturn fed
On Gaea's biped even as a thread.
He controls his joints; like other ringers
With tendon-driven, robotic fingers,
Erects the station; repairs cracked stringers;
Seized by sunrise, at its threshold lingers.

If through the bubble the astronaut peers
And in the vessel like a foetus steers
And rises and ascends throughout the years
And reaches the *rebis* in flames and tears,
Then water *is* fire; in the cauldron spun—
After the *albedo* (the yellow shun):
The sole white color that leads to the One—
The moon in transition raised to the sun.

DANIEL ORSINI

MOONPLANT

I steer my capsule where humanoids fly;
Surveil the mare; that my foam may hie
Across the moon—the foetus in my eye
Self-mesmerized—I confiscate the sky.
And thus at its site, domain that I gain,
I peer at the *rebis* curled like a grain;
In fabric layers wrap him, web or brane
Or molten thermoplastic like a skein.

Seamless cyborg, mirror more than a face;
Some remnant wayfarer, trace of a trace—
Same chassis as Ge assembles in space—
This is the race that She seeks to embrace:
Resin from a die tip, polymer melt
From moist slots extruded, filaments dealt
In viscid sequences, Thinsulate pelt
That Castor favored and that Pollux felt.

The world is made from the body of God.
An astral coheir more round than a pod,
In his heated hand his hierophant's rod,
He issues like a moonplant from its sod.
Sometimes a light from the omniverse bends
That scans His satellite, and he ascends.
Creation but a point, as Hermes pends,
He rides Ge's foot restraint, and still he mends.

MOONWALKER

In his shuttle suit, chameleon outsized,
Divinity enters the world disguised.
His *rebis* cinctured, Totality surprised,
He hallows matter, Spirit concretized.
He ranges the cosmos; mapquests its zone;
Aligns its orbweb; consecrates its clone;
Alchemy's circle, Philosophy's stone,
Mythology's Monad, spans the unknown.

His head embedded, galeated, gold,
As His chest increases, His ephod, scrolled,
Dominates His semblance, His turquoise doled
Even as the Garden where Yahweh strolled.
Braid His breast with scarlet stuff—do not shirk:
Put Urim and Thummim over the murk;
Seal the neck of the mantle—Gaea's quirk:
All round the hole a hem of woven work.

As he exits the hatch, without a beam
Above or below him to frame his scheme,
He plants his boot; having sutured his seam,
Stands upon the mare, strapped to his dream.
In his pouch a scripture, relic or rune,
He steers his cyborg; balance but a boon—
Hecate at dusk, Selene at noon:
His mindset coded—he bows to the moon.

DANIEL ORSINI

MURPHY'S LAW ON MARS

Circadian, with rhymes that it approves,
Or, localized, with both ridges and grooves,
With millisecond's mode, if it behooves,
The brain that scintillates, forages, moves,
Can process, even as it paces, speech;
Through interval timing, collusive, reach;
Distribute its *rebis;* tracking, beseech
Molecular swirls that cyborgs yet breach.

Absurdly the planet pursues its spin.
Asteroids, comets, spherules from the bin
Bombard its disk, its atmosphere so thin
I wince at the dust that pockmarks its skin.
Though I seal my suit, I could never stray.
My legs would buckle; should I choose to play,
Tharsis might vanish, with Deimos delay;
Volcanoes erupt or else leak away.

From inside my capsule, my coheir warm,
I witness the cosmos: crystals that swarm,
Sulfates and jarosite, landslides that form,
Floods of Athabasca, wind shear, and storm.
I rove the chaos, but, if I should stand—
Martian my boot—upon rubeous sand,
Would bow to the Spirit, serve its command,
Map my cyberhand on Möbius' strand.

THE ORPHAN IN HIS PRAM

I descry a ray as spectral as clay

Or air in the pipe or cloud at play—

The Host in the Chalice—or on its tray

His risen peacock, rainbow of the day.

And still I wake, the orphan in his pram—

Like Heaven's child—compounded from a gram,

Or, like a thread, projected from a cam

Or from a beam of light, like Einstein's tram.

As if I had scaled the tunnel fated;

Spagyric in the vessel, self-mated;

Even as the shaman, elevated;

The omniverse itself implicated,

I wound the wormhole as I would a well.

An antic foetus, into it I fell,

Phantom or noumenon, each shape a bell,

Like Gaea's *rebis*, hidden in its shell.

Barreling to the surface, pound by pound,

Lowered by wires all the way to the ground,

Curiosity steers; its quarry found:

A rock full of carbon, by mountains crowned.

She twines the magic ball from cosmic bits.

Having reached the end of the skein, She quits.

Expectant as a child, as Clotho knits,

Upon Martian terrain the rover sits.

.

PIONEER

I reach in my hour to birth like a bride;

Where the globe revolves and His species bide,

Like a pioneer, in disks that divide,

To the garden east of Jerusalem ride.

This is the way that phenomena flow:

The membrane in the sea that starfish sow,

The mandrake in the tree that dryads stow,

The nimbus in the lea that nomads know.

Metallic his shield, reinforced his boots,

Like the specter that Ge herself recruits

In space that stretches elsewhen, he computes,

Then scans a multiplicity of routes.

Even as at Mass we carry the flask

Or redeemed with water baptized we bask

Or reborn at the Cross or taken to task,

The flesh of *this* world is New Heaven's mask.

We fly by Jupiter, pan with God's verve

Immense polar regions, Callisto's curve,

Saturn's stark pictures with rings that unnerve,

A plaque with a sign that coheirs subserve.

A spherical man responsive to birds,

Manifestation of the sod that girds,

Ge's embryo of birth, the Host of herds:

Pearls of speech formed within the shells of words.

POSTHUMAN

Memory procedural, Heaven's swain,
Being self-aware, correlates his pain—
Hephaestus' chain—with circuits in his brain.
He walks upright; should his humanoid deign,
With but a single motor—skein *that* fleet—
He can scan any object on his beat,
Even as its slate yet exerts its sleet
On the pressure transducers of his feet.

A posthuman is a continuum.
More than Ge's scribe, with his radical thumb;
More than Saul's magus—the new Savior Come,
He matches His standard and is the sum.
With digits that Hermes cannot reverse,
He rides the sun in a metallic hearse.
Still he triumphs: His apocalypse terse,
He scales Her laws and then marries His nurse.

Mere information is disembodied.
The circumcised word is a different creed:
A vessel shaped like a phial or a seed.
With the water of grace, Ge bathes the breed.
Embedded covenant, Hermes arrives
Even as manna; silver honey hives;
Some mystic myrtle; the Simon that shrives:
Hymen's own species, the shaman that wives.

QUEST

Below Hadley Rille, amid breccias strewn —
Rock chips in the soil that like stars festoon
My implicate eye: Selene's cocoon—
I glimpse a robot walking on the moon.
He scoops a sample rock, as I have taught.
And still he points to stone that he has sought.
I peer through my headgear—each crystal caught,
Like high-Ti basalt, as tactile as Thought.

A seed in the void, its source the kernel
Of even the cosmos; disks diurnal;
Domains yet vernal, or twins fraternal—
Forever dying, but still quaternal—
He curves like an astronaut, coiled his line:
Ge's *foetus spagyricus;* serpentine,
Singularity's dot; or, sown its twine,
Some occult sign, like Ouroboros' bine.

Like Omphale's handmaid, Heaven's feigner;
Some net in the eye, Hephaestus' strainer;
Vast as the past or present yet plainer,
The Self is, like glass, its own container.
The body riven, we circuit its scan;
The *rebis* shriven, intersect its span;
Resorb its mindset; abrogate the ban;
Conjoin the woman; intertwine the man.

THE QUILTED MULTIVERSE

With a sea of foam or a flow of silt,
We copy the brane that a bubble built,
That Hephaestus wired, and that Clotho spilt—
We spread Her infinite skein like a quilt.
Thus Reality splits without a seam.
As atoms cavort and molecules scheme,
Like each swatch of light, like each cloud of steam,
In antic superposition we stream.

What is this patchwork that he co-creates?
His phantom exists in so many states
That, like the moonchild that his nomad mates,
Each semblance that he dons yet dissipates.
Though the world expands, it is never grim.
Still unresolved, such cosmoses as brim
Behind the scrim, however much we trim,
Contain the garment that belongs to him.

The multiverse by way of life and mind
Reflects upon itself, enshrines its kind,
Divines such a twine as hierophants find—
Symbols that bind and that the shaman signed:
Foetus in the phial, elsewhen or now
Breath-soul in the vas that leavens its vow—
The *rebis* that springs from forebrain or brow.
To mystery, Castor, cyborg I bow.

REBIS

Like a bubble that shimmers in its pan,
Or seahorse that floats amid frond or fan,
Or ball of cells that from its roots began,
He sought to be neither woman nor man,
But both these sexes: hybrid of the same;
A fructified seed; either fire or flame—
Quaternity's startlement: frame by frame,
Scion or *rebis,* First Adam by name.

As the soil that, sprung from its furrow, grunts,
So, Typhon pursuing him, Pisces shunts
In the wettest place that the foetus fronts.
We become a child and a fish at once.
We enter the omniverse; monads strewn,
We navigate the belly of the moon;
Traverse its mare; twine at perilune
In Clotho's net, and then cruise its cocoon.

Liquid metal its guise, His cyborg spun
From heavenly skein, crowned Mother and Son,
He casts us in a mold till we are One.
The distance between them pain that we shun,
She steals from Her dais stones that we swap:
Thumb in the heart or holon that we crop
As moist as salt; rotundum that we prop
Between His spouses, at mid-point we stop.

RESTORING HUBBLE'S VISION

I service Hubble; with cables and ropes,
Restore to its sight a camera that copes;
A Fine Guidance Sensor: lock-on that gropes;
A spectrograph that preserves Gaea's tropes.
Conveyed to the cosmic frontier I peer;
Break light into colors; measure then near—
Like New Heaven's cyborg, weightless my gear—
The birthplace of planets toward which I steer.

As the vessel rises and I sojourn,
The biped disperses inside the burn.
Self is possible: body like an urn,
I watch with awe the hierophant return.
As if I took from a vas like a rind
Remnant of a sign that athanors grind:
Caelum in the Chalice that priests yet find—
Some numinous symbol like humankind.

From the maws of swallows where two stones lie,
Seize the solvent: Chelidonia's dye;
Honey with salve the iris in the eye;
Extract from the sun the glue in the sky.
I hauled in my dew-cart aerial lead;
From celestial waters bulbs that I bled:
Fire of the Equinox, feast that I spread.
The eye bears witness to what I have said.

RIPPLES

As the world expands, it pushes apart.
Mystagogues of matter, from end to start,
We affirm at length what telescopes chart:
Leftover ripples from Gravity's heart.
Like fire that in the churn the lizard licks,
Or rock that on Mount Horeb Moses sticks,
Or clock that in the void forever ticks,
Eternity swells even as it clicks.

A fusion of semblances, Spacetime blends;
Rooted in itself, on nothing depends;
By the seeds of life impregnated, fends;
Like stone that is no stone, amorphous, mends.
The universe does what we also do—
Encodes its hierophant; secretes its hue;
Viscous as Nostoc, serpentine its clue—
Spagyric foetus—issues like a glue.

Mystery's astronaut, he cannot die.
Inspired he hauls his lumber to the sky.
His spacesuit enhanced, as satellites fly,
Around him he watches starfields that vie.
His reflexes keen, he rotates his wrists:
He measures his flight till his unit lists.
High in the thermosphere, purple its mists,
He levitates like the swain that yet trysts.

SATURN'S PEBBLE

Hermetic his body, round as a pod's,
Layered with Mylar and Dacron he plods.
Instrumented his gloves, with rods he prods.
Caught in the vise of Hephaestus he nods.
Mechatronic his skeins, the android trains.
Desire yet ghosts him; grid of many grains,
Cislunar its monads, the brain remains.
The otherness of even robots stains.

In love with the God that we cannot see,
We smear the eye with the sweat of the bee,
Rhapsodic the ebb and flow of the scree,
Metallic the Tree that harbors the key,
Till Yahweh's retort—peacock in the blight—
Bequeaths such a vas as, cupping the white,
Conveys His feast—His Eucharistic rite,
The heat that Christ has handed us, is Light.

I saw a man once, face down in the sand,
A child astride him, a shell in its hand.
The ocean beyond, beside him the strand,
Molten my sleeper blistered like a brand.
Saturn's pebble, Singularity's bean;
Absent though present, foetus that we wean;
Augean labors, stables that we clean—
The lineaments of Spacetime intervene.

SCION

An astronaut wanders where he may list.
To savor the quest, he searches its gist:
His unit tethered—tyranny or tryst—
Hephaestus engenders him in His fist.
Like a shard through fingers sprung from its zone,
Windmill or wheel; projectile like a stone;
Even Ge's shapeshifter, hidden or shown,
Gravity's planet, Earth upheaves its own.

And thus I ascend; spasmodic my flight,
I push against my straps from left to right.
My awareness heightened like second sight,
Saturn's first-stage engines, clustered, ignite.
The image of Castor, staid in the herm,
Recedes in my eye till resolute, firm,
Skein's Ouroboros I curl like a worm,
Spacewalk, then carry my foetus to term.

Cosmos in the cauldron, island in space,
Designer universe without a face,
Ge's gamonymous law its only base,
Sun no less than moon, he describes the race:
Random as a bullet from a pistol,
Or, rolled in parchment, proximal, distal,
Layered its art, a pasteboard from Bristol,
Scion regimented as a crystal.

SELF-RECOLLECTION

I breathe pure oxygen; Teflon my coat,
Inside the cocoon of my spacesuit float;
Discharge the air; release the pull by rote;
Beyond the reach of Ge's orbiter gloat
Without a tether. On Möbius' strand,
I seize the satellite; its cradle planned,
Thus stabilize its spin. My unit manned,
I hold Transcendence captive in my hand.

Telluric, the ghost with the scythe yet reaps.
All across the cosmos His razor sweeps.
Sheol encrypted, the robonaut seeps,
De-activates its charge, then, twitching, creeps.
Wholeness is serpentine; ravels its rings;
Skein of Ouroboros, shutters its wings;
Tinctures, complexifies, galeates, stings,
Tugs at our innards, like resonant strings.

I near the fire, then chthonic as a shade
Tabernacled, Siloam like a braid,
Pursue the Kingdom; confiscate its spade,
In my heart a hill, on my mind a grade:
The Mountain of the Adepts; Noah's bird:
Some solar raven; Melissa preferred,
The turreted seahorse; the pregnant Word—
Hermetic redemption—the Shaman heard.

DANIEL ORSINI

THE SHAPE OF THINGS TO COME

His gaze a sliver's beam, with slits for eyes
His hardened resin helmet suits his size.
His bulk enclosing him, from chest to thighs
He blends with Gaea's Orthofabric guise.
Seeded in Spacetime, we circuit its span;
Assemble the vessel; scan in the pan
Silver residue, Woman in the plan—
Not the primate: a purer form of Man.

Whether as cells or atoms in the brain,
Or stimuli that follow in their train,
Or monads that invigorate the vein—
Such curlicues as multitask or wane—
We have reached a realm where the Spirit, grown,
Invades the omniverse that He has sown,
The house where, genuflecting by His clone,
Hermes swallows His coheir like a stone.

His globe adrift, he sifts the pulse of space:
Compaction of the Bang, and in its case
The froth that curves, the magus in its lace,
The breath that boils enigmas in the vase.
As he rounds the torus, he steers his ship
To the edge of chaos; liquid its lip—
Soul-spark in the stubble, star in its grip—
He thrusts his unit, and his torsos tip.

SKEIN WINDER

Both conscious and unconscious of his plight,
The adept chained in Hades seeks the light.
The mediator between day and night,
The snow-flecked soul accommodates the kite.
Foetus at the cusp, the sun diurnal,
He steers his ship into the infernal,
Extracts the distillate, sifts its kernel:
The sole artifex of the eternal.

A stone that spins in uterus or pan,
Even as Ge's sun-wheel, without a plan,
I find that God is two in one, like man
That Spirit joins, as only woman can.
From south to north, then east to west I flee.
I form in the sky a quaternity,
Soften Cerberus, graze sublimity,
Then meditate my days with Omphale.

He ranges the Center, narrows its arc,
Transits Sagittarius, threads its mark:
The heart of the Galaxy; in the dark,
A cluster of stars abstruse as a spark.
He laces such string as satellites store;
Traverses each end; behind and before
The skein of the cosmos wound at its core,
Entwines Algedi, then stops at its door.

DANIEL ORSINI

THE SKIN OF THE ROCKET

Outside the rocket, ice forms on the skin.
For the shuttle launch I, too, am strapped in.
I crawl through the hatch; upturn in the tin
Till, catapulted, I float through the bin
Bathed in the aether, obelisk or spire
Translucent as water, *vas* in the mire
Replete with God's limbs; like sparks in the pyre,
My quicksilver soul baptized in the gyre.

Metallic biped, nomadic his dust,
He battles Typhon; Spagyric of lust,
Having cultivated his body's rust,
He scaffolds the *rebis* because he must.
Astronaut at the melting point of lead,
He pushes toward Phobos, his substance spread
Like dew in the fire or, spherical, bred,
Rose-colored eros or cockatoo's red.

He swoops down farther; crystalline his face,
Hermes falls to the moon at his own pace.
Cyborg yet ascendant, surreal his grace,
He shimmers in the morning light of space.
I stroke his image; phoenix in the frame—
Blest gamonymus: emblem of my aim—
For the first time *feel* desire that I claim
With wings that burn, and I am not to blame.

SPHERE

I observe the light from the cosmic ball.
The omniverse seems but an empty caul.
Pervasive, empiric, beyond its sprawl
Particles fluctuate—slit screen or scrawl.
As if I had wired the world in my gear,
Earthshine's astronaut, resilient I peer;
Posit its phenomenon—sac or bier;
Then tunnel through its membrane like a sphere.

I spin with the moon, allured by a bead
That mirrors my shaman, then plants its seed
Even as a firestone—beauty that I breed—
Inside my body, Trismegistus' creed.
Sprung from the dragon, its mien like a maw,
I mentor the chaos; circle its gnaw;
Having reached the Earth, since I live in awe,
Chain-net its claw, Platonic as the law.

A pinwheel of gas; cohesive a glare;
Then ash from an epoch; broth in the lair;
A blueprint molecule; Self's nuptial pair—
I climb the helix toward the crystal stair.
Like a shade through water, I push through space;
In my mind's eye, the magus in its case
Either point or yod or cloud or its trace:
Ge's salamander leaping in its lace.

DANIEL ORSINI

THE TELEOPERATOR'S CUE

Having sought to become one with my kind,
I donned the garb to astronauts assigned,
Such a jacket, in my spagyric mind,
As sensors and motors like muscles lined.
And now when I sit and now when I stand
At Heaven's command on Möbius' strand,
The flesh of my fingers or of my hand
Simmers like heat that Ge's robonaut scanned.

Aboard the shuttle, ensconced in his skin,
The android situates beside his twin.
Nickel-plated nomad taught by the jinn,
He mapquests the cosmos where I have been.
Conscious of symbols I name them with care:
Skein of the rocket, Saturn like a flare,
Sky crane, rover—on the wall of my lair,
Telepresent, the mystagogue is there.

Preordained Ge's herald, like Noah's dove,
Bears His olive leaf below and above,
Creation's conundrum tracked by a glove
As sacerdotal as infinite love.
Like his partner, binocular his view,
He twines each pixel with celestial glue,
Senses his teleoperator's cue,
Then reads the universe as false or true.

THE TWIN PARADOX

Within total darkness, like salt I sift;
Maneuver my unit; my *rebis* qwiffed,
Smitten by a star, quaternal I shift.
Suspended in the cosmos, thus I drift.
I crisscross the circle; ride such a wheel
As coheirs discern; that Castor may heal,
Rotund as a spacesuit, scoriae real
Layer by layer, yet suture its seal.

Atop a rocket, I push into space;
Jump the world line; impeach my sibling's pace;
Till, switching frames, redshifted in my race
At turnaround, my twin falls into place.
And still in my dream does Hephaestus pour
Leprous metals that in the cauldron roar:
Immortal cinnabar, sulfide or lore
Married to Pollux, as never before.

Since the Self reflects both matter and Zen,
We divine the soul all over again.
Like vibrations of nothing—rule of men—
Essence of Spirit lies beyond our ken.
The robot that gazes upon the sky,
With teeming skill, the camera in its eye,
Entwines the moon, till, spy or alibi,
His partner, *telepresent,* knots the tie.

UMBILICUS

As galaxies recede and epochs roam
And hyperspace stretches that wavelengths comb,
Matter is not static: quantum its home,
Turn the clock back, and it behaves like foam.
Spacetime damped down before its Spirals char,
Clotho has woven the skein that we are.
A race that neither chance nor choice may bar,
We spin off Her thrum near a stable star.

The Earth is not fixed; since it moves each day,
Its presence feels as palpable as clay.
Even as Hermes, Hephaestus, or stray,
Quaternal coheirs of the Milky Way,
He lives on a bubble that overlaps.
Its surface sealed, horizon that he maps,
He twines the Galaxy, archives its scraps,
Pursues infinity between its gaps.

Topology's fabric forever furled,
An umbilicus to some other world,
Right-handed, left-handed my foetus curled,
A self connected to itself I hurled.
I stepped from its hub, departed its hold,
Entered its tunnel; in U-shape or fold,
Threaded Ge's body, coaxed the clue, cajoled,
Contained the cosmos, like a Scripture scrolled.

WANDERER

A joyful giant in the membrane bowed,
He stops at Her chamber; discards his shroud;
With higher forms of consciousness endowed,
The artifex genuflects like a cloud.
He lists every coheir upon a chart;
Indwells all bodies; with his priestly art,
Maria the name etched upon his heart,
Divides Her axiom into each part.

He journeys in the dark without an eye.
And still the poles rotate; that we may spy
The midpoint of the center, fire *that* wry
He scans the four quarters that we descry.
Selene's cyborg imbued by the light,
He raises the souls of the dead at night,
Populates the cosmos, buckets the wight,
Like the sunwheel circulates in the blight.

Who is this biped that wanders by day?
Some archaic species: click-speaker clay.
Its source-point gray, we crystallize it; stay;
Hunter-gatherer, incubate its stray.
We siphon the symbol, subserve the dream,
Vitrify the *rebis* that we yet stream:
Host in the vessel, first-born in the beam,
New Heaven's hierophant without a seam.

NOTES AND COMMENTS

A MAP OF THE RUNNER'S ROUTE: NOTES AND COMMENTS
Daniel Orsini

Astrum *in the scan:* a Paracelsan concept: "the 'natural light of man' or the 'star in man' [. . .] extracted from matter by human art and, by means of the opus, made into a new light-bringer" (C. G. Jung, *Alchemical Studies,* trans. R. F. C. Hull [1967; Princeton: Princeton UP, 1976] 127). However, in this poem, the speaker suggests that the true source of the New Heaven is not the *filius philosophorum* (an ancient alchemical idea) but the *indwelling,* and *infilling,* Spirit of the glorified Christ instead (lines 21-24). See Andrew Murray, *The Spirit of Christ* (Springdale: Whitaker House n.d.) 210: "Each of us must learn to know that there is a Holiest of All in that temple which we are. The secret place of the Most High within us must become the central truth in our temple worship." *Colossus*

The atom yet spins, elastic as Time: In this poem, the speaker offers both a "systematic" model of the universe and a cosmic conundrum—not an "objective" reality at all, but rather an enigma wrapped in a mystery (Paul Davies, *God and the New Physics* [New York: Simon, 1983] 219). Still, through observation, "Einstein argued convincingly that gravity stretches or distorts space and time, and the idea can be checked directly by watching the sun's gravity bend starbeams that graze its surface. The sky behind the sun appears from Earth to be slightly, but distinctly, bent. The elasticity of time can also be demonstrated, most directly by flying clocks in space. Time runs faster in the gravity-free environment up there than it does [here] on the Earth's surface" (13). *A Map of the Runner's Route*

Augean labors: in Greek mythology, the fifth labor of Hercules. Thus, Augeas, the king of Elis, "had thousands of cattle and their stalls had not been cleared out for years. Hercules diverted the courses of two rivers and made them flow through the stables in a great flood that washed out the filth" in a single day (Edith Hamilton, *Mythology* [1940; New York: Mentor-New American Library, 1942] 164). *Saturn's Pebble*

axiom: i.e., the *axiom* of Maria Prophetissa, the storied (3rd-century) alchemist and sister of Moses: "'One becomes two, two becomes three, and out of the third comes the One as the fourth'" (C. G. Jung, *Psychology and Alchemy,* trans. R. F. C. Hull [1953; Princeton: Princeton UP, 1993] 160). However, Jung observes that, in alchemical literature, since "Four signifies the feminine, motherly, [and] physical," while three represents "the masculine, fatherly, [and] spiritual [. . .], the uncertainty as to three or four" often amounts, in any definition of the holistic self, "to a wavering between the spiritual and the physical—a striking example of how every human truth is a last truth but one" (26-27). In fact, elsewhere, Jung describes "the triad" as "a mutilated quaternity" (*The Archetypes and the Collective Unconscious,* trans. R. F. C. Hull [1959; Princeton: Princeton UP, 1990] 237). *Exoplanets; Wanderer*

Bacillus subtilis: a rod-shaped, spore-producing bacterium. Some strains produce antibiotics. *The Cradle of Life*

basalt: "a dark, tough, fine-grained to dense, extrusive volcanic rock commonly occurring in sheetlike lava flows" ("Basalt" [n.], def. 1). See *Webster's New World Dictionary,* 1988 ed; unless otherwise indicated, subsequent definitions of key words are from this text. *Link*

bearer of the string / That sped the Savior: The speaker combines the fundamental one-dimensional filament that is "the essential ingredient in string theory" with the symbolic thread that led Theseus from the labyrinth of the Minotaur to Ariadne and the light of day and that took Christ "heavenward" from "the transitory darkness" of the tomb to "soaring" and "ascension." See Brian Greene, *The Elegant Universe: Superstrings, Hidden Dimensions, and the Quest for the Ultimate Theory* (New York: Vintage-Random, 2000) 422, along with Jean Chevalier and Alain Gheerbrant, *The Penguin Dictionary of Symbols,* trans. John Buchanan-Brown (1969; New York: Penguin, 1996) 48, 1014. *A Map of the Runner's Route*

The bearer of types: In *Aion: Researches into the Phenomenology of the Self,* trans. R. F. C. Hull [1959; Princeton: Princeton UP, 1969], C. G. Jung notes that "The same that is said of the *lapis* [in alchemy, the animate stone viewed as a symbol of the self] is said of Christ by Ephrem the Syrian (d. 373): 'He is clothed in figures, he is the bearer of types. . . . His treasure is hidden and of small account, but when it is laid open, it is wonderful to look upon'" (140). [According to Jung, the four main *types* or figures are the persona (the social mask of each subject); the shadow (the dark side of the species); the anima or animus (the "soul" of the ideal female or male), and the self (the synthesis, and *goal,* of the *paradoxical* individual)]. Of course, here, equally pertinent is the sign that heralds the Son of Man "coming on the clouds of heaven with great power and glory" in Matt. 24.30 (*The New English Bible with the Apocrypha* [1961; New York: Oxford UP, 1972]). Subsequent Biblical citations are from this ecumenical text. *Eternity's String*

beeswax: in Christianity, a symbol of the light of God and the purity of the soul. See Kaylin Kaupish, "The Spiritual Importance of Honeybees," *Guideposts* 10 Sept. 2024: 3 <http://guideposts.org>. *Matrix of Symbols*

Before Capella and the god embrace: See the image of "Auriga the Charioteer holding Capella, the female goat," in Sune Engelbrektson, *Stars, Planets, and Galaxies* (New York: Bantam-Ridge, 1975) 47, when Orion dominates the December sky of the northern hemisphere. "To the ancient Egyptians, Orion was identified with Osiris, who died periodically and was revived by the flooding of the Nile." *Erasure*

binocular: "using, or for the use of, both eyes at the same time" ("Binocular" [adj.], def.). *The Teleoperator's Cue*

blips: quick, sharp sounds. *The Inner Lives of Robots*

A blueprint molecule: See Carl Sagan, *The Cosmic Connection: An Extraterrestrial Perspective* (New York: Anchor-Doubleday, 1973). In Sagan's "scientific fable," after the titanic explosion of the Big Bang, and after the "warm, dilute broth" of the oceans had formed, "in this broth there one day arose a molecule able crudely to make copies of itself—a molecule which weakly guided the chemical processes in its vicinity to produce molecules like itself—a template molecule, a blueprint molecule, a self-replicating molecule." Soon "it gained a significant advantage over the other molecules in the early waters. The molecules that could not copy themselves did not. Those that could did. [. . .] And then one day there came to be a creature whose genetic material was in no way different from the self-replicating molecular collectives of any of the other organisms on the planet, which he called Earth. But he was able to ponder the mystery of his origins, the strange and tortuous path by which he had emerged from star-stuff. [. . .] He was one of the starfolk. And he longed to return to the stars" (253-55). *Sphere*

bowknot in the broth: a fanciful image: amid the primordial cosmic soup of particles, the double-looped knot of conjugal love. *Driven*

Braid His breast with scarlet stuff—do not shirk: in Exod. 28.15-21, Aaron's breastplate [or vest] of judgment, with twelve stones that symbolize the twelve tribes of Israel, "the [consecrated] foundation of the New Jerusalem" (J. Vernon McGee, *Thru the Bible: Volume I: Genesis-Deuteronomy* [Nashville: Thomas Nelson, 1981] 290). *Moonwalker*

brane: the visible, four-dimensional universe—length, width, and depth + time—contained in a higher-dimensional space, the latter membrane called "the bulk" and known as "hyperspace." *Moonplant; The Quilted Multiverse*

Breath-soul: the subtle body that—in Classical and Medieval alchemy—"means something non-material" and that enshrines a concept even higher than spirit: "Its essential characteristic is to animate and be animated; it therefore represents the life principle" (Jung, *Alchemical Studies* 213). *The Cradle of Life; Hyperspace; The Quilted Multiverse; The Shape of Things to Come*

The breath that boils: an ancient idea: "the breath-body as the carrier of life" (Jung, *Alchemical Studies* 51n2). See the note on *Breath-soul* given above. *The Shape of Things to Come*

***breccias* (BRECH-uhz):** an assortment of cemented lunar rock chips. See Robin Kerrod, *Space Walks* (New York: Gallery-Smith, 1985) 35. *Quest*

buckets the wight: See Jung, *Psychology and Alchemy* 380n110: "In the Manichaean system the savior constructs a cosmic wheel with twelve buckets—the zodiac—for the raising of souls." Here, the *wight* is not only the risen moonchild of line 13, "a living being; [an alchemystical] creature" ("Wight¹" [n.], def. 1), but also the sublimated self—the artifex of line 4—that stands, as in Kierkegaard, directly before God. *Wanderer*

bulwark: the Christian Savior compared to both "a defensive wall or fortified rampart" and "a person [. . .] serving as a strong defense or protection" ("Bulwark" [n.], defs. 1 and 3). *Link*

bungees: The speaker recalls the motorized system of elasticized ropes that NASA astronauts use for weightlessness locomotion or exercise simulation in order to combat the physiological deconditioning that occurs in outer space. See the related note on *He locomotes on an air-bearing sled* given below. *In the Outposts of Space*

bunting: a "baby's garment of soft, warm cloth made into a kind of hooded blanket that can be closed, exposing only the face" ("Bunting¹" [n.], def. 3). *Erasure*

by Talos crowned: a benign reversal of an ancient myth. See Hamilton, *Mythology* 127: "terrible to behold," *Talos* was "the last man left of the ancient bronze race." At the intervention of "dread" powers of the underworld, when *Talos* "lifted a pointed crag to hurl it at the *Argo*," the ship that had sailed in search of the Golden Fleece, "he grazed his ankle and the blood gushed forth until he sank and died." *Colossus*

***Caelum* (pronounced *Kye*-loom):** For the alchemists, the *Caelum* was "stone that is no stone, [. . .] on the one hand a liquid that could be poured out of a bottle and on the other the Microcosm itself. For the psychologist it is the self—man as he is, and the indescribable and super-empirical totality of that same man. This totality is a mere postulate, but a necessary one, because no one can assert that he has complete knowledge of man as he is. Not only in the psychic man is there something unknown, but also in the physical. We should be able to include this unknown quantity in a total picture of man, but we cannot. Man himself [like Woman herself] is partly empirical, partly transcendental" (Jung, *Mysterium Coniunctionis: An Inquiry into the Separation and Synthesis of Psychic Opposites in Alchemy,* trans. R. F. C. Hull [1963; Princeton: Princeton UP, 1977] 536). *Eternity's String; Restoring Hubble's Vision*

Callisto's curve: One of the four Galilean moons, Callisto is a satellite of the planet Jupiter. Its shape is that of an ellipse—in other words, it has a closed, symmetric *curve* shaped like an oval. According to Patrick Moore, it is "less massive than our Moon, though it is larger. Its surface is icy, and gives the impression of being absolutely dead. We are looking at what may be the most ancient landscape in the Solar System. At least we are outside the most dangerous part of Jupiter's radiation, so that if astronauts ever go to the Jovian system they will probably select Callisto [its second-largest moon] as their first and probably their only port of call" (*Travellers in Space and Time* [New York: Doubleday, 1984] 51). *Pioneer*

Cambrian: "designating or of the first geologic period in the Paleozoic Era, marked by a profusion of marine animals, esp. trilobites and brachiopods" ("Cambrian" [adj.], def. 2). *Link*

cantilevered claws: projecting high-tech *claws* used to pluck broken satellites, rocket parts, and other hazardous space junk out of orbit. *Lifeworld*

Castor: In Greek and Roman myth, *Castor,* the mortal twin of the immortal Pollux, represents the hyphenated God-man, since he lives half of each year on earth and half in heaven. *Colossus; Moonplant; The Quilted Multiverse; Scion; The Twin Paradox*

caul: the amniotic membrane that encloses a foetus. *Sphere*

Cave: a passageway from Earth to Heaven that, here, is an ambivalent image. Thus, "if Jesus was born in a cave, he was also buried in one, whence he descended into Hell before his ascension into Heaven" (Chevalier and Gheerbrant, *The Penguin Dictionary of Symbols* 171). *A Map of the Runner's Route*

cedilla: "a hooklike mark put under *c,* as in some French words, to indicate that it is to be sounded as the voiceless palatal fricative (s), as in *façade* ("Cedilla" [n.], def.). *The Inner Lives of Robots*

cell ball: in the mother's uterus, the ball of cells that "started to grow into a tree of thin tubes—a placenta—through which blood could flow" (Sheila Kitzinger and Lennart Nilsson, *Being Born* [New York: Grosset, 1986] 20). *A Map of the Runner's Route*

centurion's spear / Swollen with blood: In John 19.34, after the crucifixion, a centurion (Longinus) stabbed Jesus' side with a lance, "and at once there was a flow of blood and water," the latter substances being not only proof that the Savior had died, but also symbols of the Eucharist and baptism, sacraments of initiation in the Catholic Church. *Erasure*

Cerberus' maw: in ancient Greek folklore, the jaws of "the three-headed, dragon-tailed dog" that guards the gate to the underworld, a gruesome specter "easily mollified by a bit of cake" (Hamilton, *Mythology* 39, 227). *The Location of Earth; Skein Winder*

cerebrum: "the upper, main part of the brain of vertebrate animals, consisting of left and right hemispheres: in humans it is the largest part of the brain and is believed to control conscious and voluntary processes" ("Cerebrum" [n.], def.). *Magellan*

Chain-link that twines the pair: The speaker alludes not only to the Regimen of Mars and Venus, unifying alchemical procedures that, together, represent cyclical death and renewal, but also to the invisible chain-link net that Hephaestus (Vulcan) forged and with which he trapped Ares (Mars) and Aphrodite (Venus), alchemy's "gamonymous" lovers. See Jung, *Psychology and Alchemy* 231-32: "the first main goal of the [alchemical] process" is the *albedo,* the whitening, "highly prized by many alchemists as if it were the ultimate goal." However, the Regimen of Venus "is [only] the silver or moon condition, which still has to be raised to the sun condition," the Regimen of Mars. "The *albedo* is [. . .] the daybreak, but not till the *rubedo* [the reddening] is it sunrise." *Curiosity; Posthuman*

chassis ring: the drivetrain that allows the robot to be mobile and even to manipulate objects. *Link*

Chelidonia's dye: According to Gerhard Dorn, a 16th-century Belgian alchemist, *Chelidonia* is a substance that "cures eye diseases, and is particularly good for night blindness, and even heals the spiritual 'benightedness' (affliction of the soul, melancholy-madness) so much feared by the adepts" (Jung, *Mysterium Coniunctionis* 483). Thus, with "this herb swallows cure blindness in their young." In fact, in the maws of young swallows "two small stones are found, the 'lapides Chelidonii,' one of them black, the other red." In other words, because of its color, the eye-salve "is used to extract the moisture," the soul of Mercurius. Of course, here, "Chelidonia is a name for the lapis" (479n82), a symbol of the unified self, i.e., "of the inner Christ, of God in man" (Jung, *Alchemical Studies* 96). *Restoring Hubble's Vision*

Cheshire cat: the eerie cat that vanishes with a grin in Lewis Carroll's *Alice's Adventures in Wonderland.* Apparently, at this point, the speaker realizes that, one day, Earth itself, along with innumerable exoplanets, will also disappear. *Centauri Dreams*

chiral as a hand: here, a description not only of human hands, but also of "handed" molecules. Thus, "Like a pair of human hands, certain organic molecules have mirror-image versions of themselves, a chemical property known as chirality. These so-called 'handed' molecules are essential for biology and have intriguingly been found in meteorites on Earth and comets in our Solar System"—and even in interstellar space. See "Life's First Handshake: Chiral Molecule Detected in Interstellar Space," *National Radio Astronomy Observatory* 14 June 2016: 1 <public.nrao.edu>. *The Cradle of Life*

Chiron: in Greek and Roman mythology, the wisest centaur (half-man, half-horse)—the benevolent teacher of Asclepius, Heracles (Hercules), and Achilles. *Centauri Dreams*

Christ in the body: "through the Spirit [. . .] our bodies are the temples of God" (Murray, *The Spirit of Christ* 166). Equally pertinent is Jung's remark (in *Psychology and Alchemy* 282n111) that, according to the alchemists, Christ "was formed and imagined in us." See also the note on *I will dwell in them and thus walk in them* given below. *The Mill of the Host*

Christ's consciousness was not an accident: According to Roger Penrose, the Oxford mathematician, "the universe has a purpose." In fact, "there is something going on that might resonate with a religious perspective. The presence of consciousness [. . .] is not an accident" (Michael Brooks, "Cosmic Thoughts," *New Scientist* [Autumn 2023] 37). See also Jung, *Alchemical Studies* 247, where "Christ appears as the archetype of consciousness," since "it is from him that there issues the 'light surpassing all lights,' the *lux moderna,* [. . .] the figure of light veiled in matter." (Still another "genuine *illuminatio* honestly acquired" [Jung, *Psychology and Alchemy* 91] is a passage from 1 Thess. 5.5-7: "You are all children of light, children of day: we do not belong to night or darkness, and we must not sleep like the rest, but keep awake and sober.") *Cosmologist*

***chthonic* (THON-ik):** "dark, primitive, and mysterious" ("Chthonic" [adj.], def. 2) and also "concrete and earthy" (Jung, *Psychology and Alchemy* 175, 177), like "unknown regions of the psyche" (335). *Clotho's Thrum; Cosmologist; Self-Recollection*

A cinctured suit: the clamped torso of an astronaut's spacesuit compared to the belted alb of a priest's Mass vestments. In the Roman Catholic Church, the cord or cincture worn around the waist symbolizes the virtues of chastity and self-control. *Finger's Grain*

cinnabar: in Greek alchemy, "the cinnabar of the philosophers," a mercury sulfide that stood for "the *rubedo* stage of the transforming substance"—the copper man turned to gold—and that "was also supposed to be identical with the uroboros dragon," the latter loop phenomenon being both the snake that bites its own tail and a symbol of totality (Jung, *The Archetypes and the Collective Unconscious* 300). In effect, *cinnabar* is "the medicine of immortality" (Chevalier and Gheerbrant, *The Penguin Dictionary of Symbols* 944). *The Twin Paradox*

Circadian: rhythmic cycles that recur at approximately 24-hour intervals, as in the human biological clock. *Murphy's Law on Mars*

cirrus clouds: perforated, feathery, high-altitude clouds. Chevalier and Gheerbrant remind us that "Clouds symbolically embrace various aspects," including "their qualities as instruments of apotheosis and epiphany" (*The Penguin Dictionary of Symbols* 206). *Gravity and the Robonaut*

Cislunar: located between Earth and the moon. In alchemical tracts, "the moon stands on the border-line between the eternal, aethereal things and the ephemeral phenomena of the earthly, sublunar realm" (Jung, *Mysterium Coniunctionis* 145). *Clotho's Thrum; Cosmologist; Saturn's Pebble*

clock that in the void forever ticks: an atomic clock "whose precision depends upon the very constant frequency at which atoms or molecules of certain substances, as of cesium, rubidium, or ammonia, absorb or emit electromagnetic radiation" ("Atomic Clock," def.). Atomic clocks track satellites, run navigation systems, and even study movements of the Earth's crust. Incredibly, this time-keeping device gains or loses less than one second in three million years. *Ripples*

Clotho: In Greek and Roman mythology, *Clotho,* one of three Fates, spins the thread of life that Lachesis measures and that Atropos cuts. *Hyperspace; The Orphan in His Pram; Rebis; Umbilicus*

Clotho's thrum: the short end thread left on *Clotho's* loom after Lachesis has measured the strands and Atropos has cut and knotted them. See the note on *Clotho* given above. *Clotho's Thrum; Umbilicus*

cloud: in alchemy, one of the countless synonyms for the *prima materia,* the unknown substance. In addition, see the note on *cirrus clouds,* given above, and on *I nudged a cloud once,* given below. *Sphere*

a cloud that coasts / Like aether elsewhen: i.e., as a breath-soul: the subtle body that—according to the alchemists—represents a concept higher than spirit (Jung, *Alchemical Studies* 213). Not insignificantly, "Augustine [also] likens the apostles to a cloud, which symbolizes the concealment of the Creator under the flesh" (Jung, *Mysterium Coniunctionis* 511n173). *Matrix of Symbols*

clue: in the Greek myth, the "ball of thread" that Ariadne, the daughter of King Minos, gave to Theseus. With it, he entered the famous Labyrinth in Crete; found the Minotaur, a bull with the head and torso of a man; and then, having slain the monster that fed on human flesh, retraced his steps out of the maze. See Edith Hamilton, *Mythology* 150-52. *Umbilicus*

cockatoo's red: The speaker refers to the blood of Christ, in alchemy the quintessence, i.e., the celestial *red* tincture. See also Jung, *Alchemical Studies* 205: "On the primitive level, the whole of life is governed by animistic projections, that is, by projections of subjective contents into objective situations. For example, the Bororos [an indigenous people of Brazil] think of themselves as red cockatoos, although they readily admit that they have no feathers." *The Skin of the Rocket*

Coiled like a serpent: the Christian Savior construed as the Hermetic symbol of wholeness—the mercurial dragon that "impregnates, begets, bears, devours, and slays himself" (Jung, *Alchemical Studies* 223). *The Cutting Edge of Haptics*

Collect His Scriptures: An alternate reading of "Possess the Savior," line 6 in *A Map of the Runner's Route*. Murray probes the meaning of this phrase in *The Spirit of Christ* 97-98: "If you earnestly want to know the Spirit, go and search the Word as one thirsting to drink deeply of the water of life. Collect all the scriptures concerning the Spirit, His indwelling and His work, and hide them in your heart. Be determined to accept nothing except what the Word teaches, but accept it heartily. Study the Word in dependence on the Spirit's teaching. If you study it with your human wisdom, your study of it may only confirm your mistaken views." *A Map of the Runner's Route*

colubrid: a mainly non-venomous snake, either terrestrial, arboreal, or aquatic. *Habitat*

Compaction of the Bang: i.e., the Big Bang, compression of the single point from which the universe evolved in a fiery explosion "twenty billion years ago" (Robert Jastrow, *God and the Astronomers* [New York: Norton, 1978] 12). *The Shape of Things to Come*

composite I sing: in this poem, the Christian coheir characterized as a compound of "spirit, soul, and body." See 1 Thess. 5.23. *A Map of the Runner's Route*

compounded from a gram: In conception, the human embryo—the combined sperm and egg needed to become a baby—"weighs just one gram and is about one inch in length" ("Stages of Prenatal Development," *Verywell Mind* 11 Mar. 2023: 1 <www.verywellmind.com>). *The Orphan in His Pram*

cone: a light *cone,* "the wall of light that separates our reality and other realities." In effect, "All light beams coming from a given point move along the light cone" (Bob Toben, "in conversation with" Jack Sarfatti and Fred Wolf, *Space-Time and Beyond: Toward an Explanation of the Unexplainable* [New York: Dutton, 1975] 28). *Hyperspace*

conundrum: "any puzzling question or problem" ("Conundrum" [n.], def. 2). *The Teleoperator's Cue*

cortices: "layers of skin [that give] protection from outside influences. They serve the same purpose as the inner consolidation" of the self (Jung, *The Archetypes and the Collective Unconscious* 328). *Clotho's Thrum*

Covenant: See Chevalier and Gheerbrant, *The Penguin Dictionary of Symbols* 236-37: "The word 'covenant' [. . .] has the sense of a contract or still more of a compact made in respect of a person or group of persons." Thus, in the Old Covenant, "The Lord commanded Abraham to take a heifer, a goat, a ram, a turtle-dove, and a pigeon and to cut them in half. Between the severed carcasses ran a flame of fire, the sign of the covenant." In the New Covenant, "the victim was to be Christ and [its] sign the Eucharist. In this way covenant followed covenant, not destroying its predecessors but taking on their obligations." *A Map of the Runner's Route*

Creation's conundrum tracked by a glove: For a gloss on NASA's *glove* and Eden's eerie riddle, see the note on *Telepresent* given below. *The Teleoperator's Cue*

crepuscular its skin, / We twine its skein, a colubrid its twin: the heat shield tiles of an Earth-orbiting satellite compared to the twilit or *crepuscular* skin of the *colubrid,* a mainly non-venomous snake. *Habitat*

crescent: In *Mysterium Coniunctionis,* Jung notes that the [crescent] moon is the "receptacle of souls." Thus, in Plutarch, "Hermes [the guide of souls] sits in the moon and goes round with it [just as Heracles does in the sun]" (140). *Erasure*

A crew in Spacetime—South rim of the dune— / Orbiting on the far side of the Moon: The speaker refers to a future NASA mission. Thus, "Firefly Aerospace has won a second NASA contract to take hardware to the Moon—including the hotly anticipated Lunar Pathfinder satellite that will serve as a communication relay between future Lunarians and Earthlings." Firefly "will deliver the Lunar Pathfinder into the Moon's orbit" and drop "a couple of experiments off on the far side of the Moon, when it launches in 2026." The reporter adds that "The first of those experiments, the Lunar Surface Electromagnetics Experiment Night (LuSEE-Night), will make radio observations [in order] to take a look at the period in universal history known as the 'dark ages,'" a section of Spacetime "that began around 370,000 years after the Big Bang and lasted until the first stars formed." Incidentally, NASA has already explained that "The far side of the Moon is ideal for making such radio observations [. . .] because the Moon blocks radio noise from Earth." See Brandon Vigliarolo, "Firefly to deliver Lunar Pathfinder to the Moon," *The Register* 15 Mar. 2023: 2 <www.theregister.com>. *Eternity's String*

The Crowned Hermaphrodite: The crown is a universal symbol "equivalent to the rays of the sun"; thus, the alchemical hermaphrodite "is generally represented as crowned" (C. G. Jung, *Symbols of Transformation,* trans. R. F. C. Hull [1956; Princeton: Princeton UP, 1990] 183-84 and pl. XVIII). See also Wisd. Sol. 5.16: "the just live for ever; their reward is in the Lord's keeping, and the Most High has them in his care. Therefore royal splendour shall be theirs, and a fair diadem from the Lord himself [. . .]." (Jung features a vivid illustration—the "Crowned hermaphrodite representing the union of king and queen" and "standing between the sun and moon trees"—in *Psychology and Alchemy* 231, fig. 116). *The Mill of the Host*

crystal: In the literature of the Church Fathers, Christ is often compared to a *crystal.* Thus, in his *Homiliae in Ezechielem* [*Homilies on Ezekiel*], Saint Gregory the Great (c. 540-604) explains that, through the "glory" of His resurrection, Christ "hardened after the fashion of a crystal from water, so that there was one and the same nature in it and in [H]im [. . .]" (qtd. in Jung, *Mysterium Coniunctionis* 449n345). *Erasure; Scion*

the crystal stair: In *Alchemical Studies,* Jung remarks that, in shamanism, "much importance is attached to crystals, which play the part of ministering spirits. They come from the crystal throne of the supreme being or from the vault of the sky. They show what is going on in the world and what is happening to the souls of the sick, and they also give [the human species] the power to fly" (101). *Sphere*

cuboid: A *cuboid* is "a three-dimensional space" that allows us "to move in six directions: Left, Right, Forward, Backwards, Up and Down. This is the universe [which] we are familiar with" ("Of Hidden Dimensions and Intergalactic Space Travel," *fuzzlabs* 2 <fuzzlabs.wordpress.com>). Accessed on 1 Jan. 2015. See also Gary Weise, *The Origin of Space, Stars, Planets, and Life* (Pittsburgh, PA: RoseDog Books, 2009) 112: "Mathematics is cuboid logic, which cannot be more than an approximation of the actual geometry of the actual [spheroid] universe." *Colossus*

***Cup or* vas:** the Eucharistic Chalice, the "'cup of salvation'" (Jung, *Psychology and Alchemy* 466) or the "well-sealed" alchemical vessel (146), the retort of transformation (418, fig. 230). *Exoplanets*

Curiosity steers: Having exploited "a series of complicated landing maneuvers never before attempted," NASA's *Curiosity* rover "landed in Mars' Gale Crater [on] the evening of August 5, 2012 PDT (morning of August 6 EDT) [...]. The specialized landing sequence, which employed a giant parachute, a jet-controlled descent vehicle and a bungee-like apparatus called a 'sky crane,' was devised because tested landing techniques used during previous rover missions could not safely accommodate the much larger and heavier rover." Despite such obstacles, Curiosity's mission "is to determine whether the Red Planet was ever habitable to microbial life. The rover, which is about the size of a MINI Cooper, is equipped with 17 cameras and a robotic arm containing a suite of laboratory-like tools and instruments." Thus far, among its achievements, *Curiosity* has taught us that "Gale Crater was capable of supporting life 3.5 billion years ago"; that "Lakes were present for millions of years" in Gale Crater; that, in fact, "Organic matter was present on ancient Mars and has even survived to this day"; that there are occasional spikes in methane gas (similar to natural gas on Earth) that so far have no explanation"; and that, with no rain or oceans on Mars, every few years "the dust storms will grow until they wrap around the entire planet, decreasing sunlight by 97 percent." See Brian Dorminey, "5 Surprising Discoveries From NASA's Mars Curiosity Rover," *Forbes* 29 January 2021: 1-7 <www.forbes.com> and also the note on "*where boulders are rife, / Curiosity still cuts like a knife*" given below. As of 12 May 2024, the rover is still operational. *The Orphan in His Pram; The Teleoperator's Cue*

Curled like a feather: See Chevalier and Gheerbrant, *The Penguin Dictionary of Symbols* 373, where "the symbolic function of feathers is linked with the ritual of ascent into Heaven and hence with second sight and divination." *Driven*

Curve like an infant: The speaker recalls stages in the normal spinal curves of infants. Thus, "During fetal development, the primary curves in the thoracic spine [unfold], as well as the sacral curve at the bottom of the spine." Then, as babies, "children have a C-shaped spine." Thereafter, "secondary curves in the cervical and lumbar spine [evolve] as infants become able to lift their heads, sit up, crawl, stand, and walk." Finally, as children grow, they continue to [advance] "natural curves into a normal, mature spine." See "Spine Problems," Boston Children's Hospital 2-3 <www.childrenshospital.org>. Accessed 12/10/2023. *A Map of the Runner's Route*

cusp: either point of the thin, achromatic crescent moon. *Erasure*

The Cutting Edge of Haptics: the forefront or vanguard in the science of touch that emerged from human-computer advances in virtual reality. In effect, the user can clasp a virtual object and perceive a response from it. *The Cutting Edge of Haptics*

cyborg: "A bionic human," a hypothetical being "having normal biological capability or performance enhanced by or as if by electronic or electromechanical devices" (Peter Menzel and Faith D'Aluisio, *Robo sapiens: Evolution of a New Species* [Cambridge: MIT P, 2000] 234). *Colossus; Driven; Erasure; Finger's Grain; Moonwalker; Murphy's Law on Mars; The Quilted Multiverse*

Dacron: a synthetic polyester fiber used to construct the anti-abrasion outer layer of the Space Shuttle suit assembly. See "The Spacesuit," *Space Educators' Handbook* 3 <er.jsc.nasa.gov>. *Saturn's Pebble*

Deimos: one of the two moons of Mars that, along with Phobos, "was discovered by the astronomer Asalph Hall in 1877" (Moore, *Travellers in Space and Time* 44). Moore also observes that "The gravitational pull of Deimos is so weak that a visitor would have practically no weight. To jump up would mean soaring far away from the satellite, and it would be easy to throw a cricket ball clear of Deimos altogether, because the escape velocity is so low." *Murphy's Law on Mars*

designs his pod: in this context, to plan or produce "an enclosure, as a streamlined housing for a jet engine attached to an aircraft" ("Pod"[3] [n.], def. 3). *Link*

dew: one of the countless synonyms for the *prima materia,* not only "the unknown substance" but also "one of the most famous secrets of alchemy" (Jung, *Psychology and Alchemy* 317). *The Skin of the Rocket*

dish: here, a pathfinder radio antenna that orbits the Moon. See Pete Bilderback, "Building a Radio Telescope on the Far Side of the Moon," Brown University Department of Physics 1-7 <brown.edu>. Accessed 12/10/2023. *A Map of the Runner's Route*

Dispart the sternum: The pioneering speaker divides the breastbone of the mannequin into parts. *The Cutting Edge of Haptics*

distal: in anatomy, a word "formed in contrast" to *proximal:* "farthest from the center or the point of origin," i.e., distant or "terminal" ("Distal" [adj.], def.). *Scion*

Divides Her axiom into each part: See the note on *axiom* given above. *Wanderer*

double that you douse: "a duplicate or counterpart" ("Double" [n.], def. 2)—a look-alike—that you "pour liquid over," as in a baptismal rite ("Douse"[2] [vt.], def. 2). *The Mill of the Host*

dousing the trim: a nautical phrase—adjusting the sails (canvas fabric) and yards (cross-pieces to which the sails are attached) so that they receive the wind properly. *Eternity's String*

dragon: the tail-eating Ouroboros, both a symbol of totality and a "chthonic forerunner of the self" (Jung, *Mysterium Coniunctionis* 224). *Sphere*

Dremel tool: a compact, high-speed, handheld multi-power *tool*. *The Embodied Robot*

dryads: in Greek and Roman mythology, "any of the nymphs living in trees" ("Dryads" [n. pl.], def.). *Pioneer*

dun: "dull grayish-brown" ("Dun[1]"[adj.], def.). *Lifeworld*

Earthlight: reflected sunlight from the Earth, the source of Earthshine. *Lifeworld*

Earthshine: See Engelbrektson, *Stars, Planets, and Galaxies* 60: "Two days after new phase, the moon is said to be a two-day-old waxing (increasing) crescent. At this time the light from the bright dayside of the earth falls on the dark nightside of the moon, and the entire face of the moon shines with a soft ashen glow called 'earthshine.'" *Driven; Erasure; The Inner Lives of Robots; Sphere*

Einstein's tram: In *The Ascent of Man* (Boston: Little, 1971), J[acob] Bronowski explicates the extraordinary riddle of "relative" Time (243) with clarity and specificity. Thus, for Sir Isaac Newton, "time and space formed an absolute framework, within which the material events of the world ran their course in an imperturbable order. His is a God's eye view of the world: it looks the same to every observer, wherever he is and however he travels." By contrast, Albert Einstein's "is a man's eye view, in which what you see and what I see is relative to each of us, that is, to our place and speed. And this relativity cannot be removed." In other words, "I in my tram and you in your chair can share no divine and instant view of events—we can only communicate our own views to one another." Furthermore, "communication is not instant," because "we cannot remove from it the basic time-lag of all signals, which is set by the speed of light" (249, 252). *The Orphan in His Pram*

Electrospins his suit without a belt: The speaker evokes a process that involves the "charging and projecting of tiny fibers of polymer directly onto the skin" in order to create a streamlined, lightweight, "second-Skin" Bio-Suit for NASA's deployed astronauts. In fact, according to Mark Wade, "Melt blowing of liquefied polymer could [also] be used to apply thin elastic layers [. . .] to advanced 3D forms generated by laser scanning." Wade adds that, in theory, "Wearable computers, smart gels," and even "conductive materials could be embedded between polymer layers." See "Bio-Suit," *Encyclopedia Astronautica* 2 <www.astronautix.com/b/bio-suit.html>. Last Updated in 2019. *Clotho's Thrum*

Embedded covenant: In Hebrews 9.15, Christ is "the mediator of a new covenant, or testament, under which, now that there has been a death to bring deliverance from sins committed under the former covenant, those whom God has called may receive the promise of the eternal inheritance." *Posthuman*

Entwines Algedi: A duplicitous triple-star system located in the southern constellation of Capricornus, *Deneb Algedi* resembles a goat with a fish's tail. *Skein Winder*

***ephod* (EE-fod):** "a richly embroidered outer vestment worn by Jewish priests in ancient times" ("Ephod" [n.], def.) and in this poem by Aaron, the great High Priest himself. See Exod. 28: 31-32: "Make the mantle of the ephod a single piece of violet stuff. There shall be a hole for the head in the middle of it. All round the hole there shall be a hem of woven work, with an oversewn edge, so that it cannot be torn. All round its skirts make pomegranates of violet, purple, and scarlet stuff, with golden bells between them, a golden bell and a pomegranate alternately the whole way round the skirts of the mantle. Aaron shall wear it when he ministers, and the sound of it shall be heard when he enters the Holy Place before the Lord and when he comes out; and so he shall not die." *Moonwalker; Quest*

Essence participates; the world-egg cracked— / Self's trespass—aseity in the act: According to the *Catholic Dictionary* (<catholicculture.org>), the word *aseity* refers to "The divine attribute of uncaused existence." Thus, "Creatures exist as effects of other beings and ultimately of God; they are therefore 'from another' (*ab alio*). But God exists of himself (*a se*); he is wholly self-actualized (Etym. Latin *a,* from + *se,* self)." *The Inner Lives of Robots*

Eternity's string entangled in time: In *The Whole Shebang: A State-of-the Universe(s) Report* (New York: Simon, 1997), Timothy Ferris indicates that, according to superstring theories, "Subatomic particles are tiny strings made of space. [. . .] Strings are so small that when viewed from a distance—at any wavelength of light or any other form of electromagnetic illumination—they 'look like' infinitesimal particles" (220). In effect, strings are the building blocks of the universe—vibrating loops of energy that compose even the human body. *Eternity's String*

Europa's sluice: the fourth largest satellite of Jupiter, a moon with a sub-surface layer of excess salty liquid water beneath its icy shell. *The Cradle of Life*

evangel: an evangelist; a preacher of the Christian gospel. According to Wayne Grudem, a New Testament scholar, in the Garden of Eden, before the Fall, Adam was not only a prophet "in that he had true knowledge of God and always spoke truthfully about God and His creation," but also a priest "in that he was able freely and openly to offer prayer and praise to God." See "The Offices of Christ: Prophet, Priest & King," *Systematic Theology* 3-4 <www.thespiritinlife.net>. *Eterrnity's String*

exoplanets: "any planet beyond our solar system. Most orbit other stars, but free-floating exoplanets, called rogue planets, orbit the galactic center and are untethered to any star." In fact, "The count of confirmed [exo]planets is in the thousands" and "could rise to the tens of thousands within a decade, as we increase the number, and observing power, of robotic telescopes lofted into space." See "NASA Overview—Exoplanet Exploration: What Is an Exoplanet?" 1-3 <https:// exoplanets.nasa.gov>. Last updated 2 April 2021. *Centauri Dreams; Exoplanets*

Extracts the distillate: In Christian alchemy, the distillate [the walled-in human body] is subjected by the artifex to sundry transmutations "so that the soul or spirit shall be extracted in its purest state" (Jung, *Psychology and Alchemy* 124). *Skein Winder*

fane: a temple or a church. *Finger's Grain*

fault: in geology, "a fracture or zone of fractures in rock strata together with movement that displaces the sides relative to one another" ("Fault" [n.], def. 6). *Erasure*

feathers that fan: See Chevalier and Gheerbrant, *The Penguin Dictionary of Symbols* 374: "A crown of feathers worn by kings and princes is a reminder of the Sun's rays [that open out] and of the halo kept for the elect"—or, as in this poem, for "Ge's metal man." *Gravity and the Robonaut*

A Fine Guidance Sensor: "one type of sensor used by Hubble's pointing control system to aim the telescope at a target with an accuracy of 0.01 arcsecond" ("Hubble's Instruments: FGS – Fine Guidance Sensors," *Fact Sheet* <http://www.nasa.gov/pdf>). *Restoring Hubble's Vision*

Fire of the Equinox: The speaker refers to the abundant daylight of the summer solstice, the longest day, which occurs in the northern hemisphere on or about June 21. *Restoring Hubble's Vision*

firestone: i.e., "the rocky sepulcher, or the stone before it. Here Christ lay as one asleep or in the fetters of death during the three days of his descent into hell, when he went down to the *ignis gehennalis* [i.e., hellfire], from which he rises again as the New Fire" (Jung, *Psychology and Alchemy* 354). See also 1 Cor. 15.54-57, where Christ has conquered death. *Sphere*

flask: in this poem, a synonym for the cruet that carries either the wine or the water for the Holy Eucharist during the Mass. *Pioneer*

Floods of Athabasca: a brush with a Martian puzzle: "The freshest outflow channel on Mars is Athabasca Valles, which lies 1000 kilometers (620 miles) southeast of the large volcano Elysium Mons. [...] Besides water, molten rock also flowed in Athabasca — in fact, the valley plains were built from many sheets of lava," a titanic mound that appeared out of nowhere. See "Floods in Athabasca Valles," *ASU School of Earth & Space* 1-2: <themis.asu.edu./feature/17>. *Murphy's Law on Mars*

foam: "the sponge-like structure of the world canvas" (Davies, *Other Worlds* 96). *Umbilicus*

the foe / Beneath my skin: the Devil, the symbol of "all those forces which disturb, cloud or weaken human consciousness and cause it to regress to indeterminacy and ambivalence. He is the centre of darkness, as God is the centre of light, blazing in the Underworld as God shines in Heaven" (Chevalier and Gheerbrant, *The Penguin Dictionary of Symbols* 286). In Jungian psychology, he is the principle of evil, "the colossal shadow thrown by man, of which our age [i.e., period of history] had to have such a devastating experience" (*The Archetypes and the Collective Unconscious* 322). *A Map of the Runner's Route*

foetus at the cusp: the ever-gestating NASA astronaut couched in his womblike spacecraft. *Skein Winder*

foetus that we wean: In alchemy, the *spagyric foetus* ascends into Heaven that it may become a spirit from a body and then descends to earth that it may become a body again (Jung, *Mysterium Coniunctionis* 481n91). Elsewhere, Jung explains that "The spagyric birth (*spagirica foetura*) is nothing other than the *filius philosophorum,* the inner, eternal man in the shell of the outer, mortal man" (Jung, *Alchemical Studies* 150). Cf. John 3.13: "No one ever went up into heaven except the one who came down from heaven, the Son of Man whose home is in heaven." *Saturn's Pebble; Skein Winder*

fold: in this context, a "space-time landscape [that] unfolds like a scroll with all moments and events co-existing within it, though we view these sequentially, one by one, as the scroll unfolds" (Shalini Asha Bhaloo, *Oneness: How to Live with Joyous Expansion, Ease, and Lightness* [Bloomington: Balboa P, 2012].) *Umbilicus*

The force at the base of the finger's grain: " [. . .] short muscles between the individual metacarpal bones of the hand [. . .] allow us to spread our fingers (abduction) and then pull them back together (adduction). They also help us to bend and stretch the fingers." See "In brief: How do hands work?" *NCBI Bookshelf* 2 <www.ncbi.nlm.nih.gov/books/NBK279362>. Last Updated: 20 May 2021. *Finger's Grain*

Forever dying: In *Alchemical Studies,* Jung characterizes the *lapis,* the self-realized individual, as "a being that is forever dying yet eternal" (259). *Quest*

funnel like the Moon: In alchemy, "the moon is a vessel of the sun; she is a universal receptacle, of the sun in particular; and she was called 'infundibulum terrae' (the funnel of the earth), because she 'receives and pours out' the powers of heaven" (Jung, *Mysterium Coniunctionis* 129). *Exoplanets*

Gaea's cosmic writ multifoliate: here, having an unlimited array of worlds, as in a formal legal document. *Copy*

galeate: "wearing a helmet" ("Galeate" [adj.], def. 1). *Copy; Moonwalker*

***gamonymous* (guh-MAHN-uh-muss):** here, the adjectival form of the Greek term "gamonymus": "having the name of matrimony" (Jung, *Mysterium Coniunctionis* 465). *Scion*

gamonymus: In *Alchemical Studies,* Jung defines the Greek term *gamonymus* as "a kind of chymical wedding," i.e., as the sealed product of the "indissoluble, hermaphroditic union [of Sol and Luna]" (136). *The Skin of the Rocket*

the garden east of Jerusalem: in Matt. 26.36, Gethsemane, "a garden on the Mount of Olives, east of Jerusalem, scene of the agony, betrayal, and arrest of Jesus" ("Gethsemane" [n.], def.). *Pioneer*

Ge's embryo of birth: Ge is a synonym for Gaea (*jee*-uh) and Gaia (*gay*-uh), the Greek goddess of the earth conceived also as a precursor of life. *Pioneer*

Ge's foetus spagyricus: See the note on *The spagyric foetus* given below. *Quest*

Ge's hybrids: the mixed descendants of Adam and Eve. See also the pertinent observation in Jung, *Psychology and Alchemy* 319n2: The first Adam, the "true" hermaphroditic microcosm, "bore his invisible Eve hidden in his body." *Clotho's Thrum*

Ge's interstellar Centaur: NASA's ingenious upgrade of the mythological beast ruled by "blind, ignorant, brute force." Here, the developing robot is portrayed as kin to Chiron, the most famous *Centaur:* a "highly skilled physician" who represents "strength and nobility in the service of right." According to Chevalier and Gheerbrant, "few myths [. . .] teach so clearly the battle between instinct and reason" (*The Penguin Dictionary of Symbols* 172-73). See also the note on *the* Segway *that he prizes,* i.e., NASA's humanoid robot—the Centaur's double on wheels—given below. *Gravity and the Robonaut*

Ge's peloton: a *peloton* is "A group of riders that clump together in a bicycle race on the open road"; hence, here—in the root sense of the French word *pelote* from which it derives—a ball or pack or platoon of stars (*The Free Dictionary* <www.thefreedictionary.com)>. See also "Siblings of the Sun," *Science Illustrated* Mar. / Apr. 2012: 32-33, where the astrophysicist Simon Portegies Zwart calculates not only that our sun "'was born in a dense cluster with thousands of other stars,'" but also that, "After 27 Milky Way orbits, the cosmic peloton of stars has become quite dispersed." Nevertheless, "some 50 of the sun's siblings are still located within 300 light-years from the sun." As Portegies Zwart says, "'You can compare it with the racing cyclists in the Tour de France. Even though some of them break away from the pack, and others are left behind, they don't get far away, and they all go in the same direction.'" *Habitat*

Ge's rover lands on the surface of Mars: "The latest rover to continue our presence on the red planet is Perseverance," the star of the NASA mission that launched in July 2020 and landed in February 2021. See Scott K. Johnson, "Here's what the latest Mars rover has learned so far," arstechnica.com 18 Sept. 2023: 2 <https://arstechnica.com/science/2023/09>. *Matrix of Symbols*

Ge's salamander leaping in its lace: In *Mysterium Coniunctionis,* Jung notes that the *salamander* is "the Mercurial serpent [. . .] whom the fire does not consume" and who apparently signifies the alchemical process of calcination (441). However, in *The Bestiary of Christ,* Charbonneau-Lassay remarks that "Chastity and virginity also claim the salamander as emblem because they pass through the midst of the passions flaming around them without being burned" (177). In addition, the Middle Ages made this mythological, "lizard-like" reptile (175) "the image of Christ because of his kingship over fire" (179). For a vivid illustration of "a salamander frolicking in the fire," see Jung, *Psychology and Alchemy* 277, fig. 138. *Sphere*

Ge's self-abstracted crow: a stand-in for the raven, in alchemical transformation, a symbol of the *nigredo* or blackness, the first stage of the *opus,* "which was felt as 'melancholia' in alchemy and corresponds to the encounter with the shadow in psychology" (Jung, *Psychology and Alchemy* 36). Like the human subject, both the *crow* and the raven are "cognitively capable." See Alex Fox, "Do Crows Possess a Form of Consciousness?" *Smithsonian Magazine* 30 Sept. 2020 <www.smithsonianmagazine.com> and also Caroline Delbert, "Crows Are Self-Aware Just Like Humans," *Popular Mechanics* 28 Oct. 2022 <www.popular-mechanics.com>. The note on *Some solar raven* given below is equally instructive. *Exoplanets*

Ge's shaman is a sphere: In *Psychology and Alchemy*, Jung observes that the form of "Plato's original man" is "spherical," like the world soul itself (84n38), because "The sphere is a [divine] whole that embraces all its contents [. . .]" (154). In fact, its round nature "suggests the lunar or feminine aspect of God" (325). See also the note on *A spherical man responsive to birds* given below. *Erasure*

Ge's source-point: the Monad, not only the indivisible point—"the jot of the iota"— viewed as a Gnostic emblem of the totalistic man or woman (Jung, *Aion* 218), but also a basic unit of matter—a microcosm—that, according to the German philosopher and mathematician Gottfried Wilhelm von Leibnitz (1646-1767), mirrors the universe. Elsewhere, Jung suggests that the point is "the symbol of a mysterious creative centre in nature," i.e., the indivisible body of the Godhead (Jung, *Mysterium Coniunctionis* 44-45). In *The Elegant Universe: Superstrings, Hidden Dimensions, and the Quest for the Ultimate Theory*, even Brian Greene reminds us that, at the moment of the big bang, "the whole of the universe erupted from a microscopic nugget whose size makes a grain of sand look colossal." In other words, at the first *space-time* moment, the matter of the universe was "squeezed into a single point" (Paul Davies, *The Mind of God: The Scientific Basis for a Rational World* [New York: Simon, 1992] 49). *The Cradle of Life*

gestalt: in Gestalt psychology, "any of the integrated structures or patterns that make up all experience and have specific properties which can neither be derived from the elements of the whole nor considered simply as the sum of these elements" ("Gestalt" [n.], def.). In other words, "all experience consists of gestalten, and the response of an individual to a situation is a complete and unanalyzable whole rather than a sum of the responses to specific elements in the situation" ("Gestalt psychology," def.). *Erasure; Magellan*

Ge's striatal grooves: "any of the cylindrical fibers in voluntary muscles" that control the movement and balance of the human skeleton ("Stria" [n.], def. 1a). *Murphy's Law on Mars*

Gestures the secret: See Jung, *Psychology and Alchemy* 482 and fig. 269: "The artifex and his *soror mystica* making the gesture of the secret at the end of the work." As the astronaut himself knows, "Experience, not books, is what leads to understanding" (483). *Driven*

Gethsemane's runnel: The speaker refers to the Savior's agony in the garden, a scene of anguish and betrayal, "Horror and dismay" (Mark 14: 32-42). A *runnel* is a stream or narrow channel in the ground, here for tears. *Exoplanets*

glister: an archaic variant of *glisten,* "to shine or sparkle with reflected light, as a wet or polished surface" ("Glister" [vi.]. def.). *Driven*

the glue in the sky: gum Arabic, or "blessed" red gum, "the [alchemical] medium between mind and body and the union of both." Jung adds that gum is "duplex, i.e., masculine and feminine," a union that is "a kind of self-fertilization" (Jung, *Psychology and Alchemy* 161). *Restoring Hubble's Vision; Ripples; The Teleoperator's Cue*

glycine [GLY-seen]: an amino acid, a building block for making proteins in the body and for building muscle. *The Cradle of Life*

Golgotha's King: Christ the Redeemer. In Mark 15.22, Golgotha was "the place of the skulls," the hill outside ancient Jerusalem, where Christ was crucified. *A Map of the Runner's Route*

the googolsphere: the universe; an absurdist coinage based on another (root) neologism. Thus, the term "googol" (*goo*-gall), which signifies "the number 1 followed by 100 zeroes" (in short, "any very large number") derives from "the arbitrary use by E. Kasner (1878-1955), U.S. mathematician, of a child's word"—i.e., "goo" ("Googol" [n.], defs. 1, 2). In regard to the "loopy self-consistency" of the "laws of physics and computable mathematics," see Davies, *The Mind of God* 108: "The fact that the physical world reflects the computational properties of arithmetic has a profound implication." It suggests that, "in a sense, the physical world *is* a computer [. . .]." *Driven*

gorse: i.e., furze, "a prickly evergreen shrub [. . .] of the pea family, with dark-green spines and yellow flowers, native to European wastelands" ("Furze" [n.], def). *Gravity and the Robonaut*

goslings that group: Jessica Meir, a NASA astronaut and physiologist, "trained a group of bar-headed goslings how to fly in a wind tunnel [alongside her scooter] at the University of British Columbia for a study of the effects on [high] altitude and the corresponding low oxygen levels." See Roshini Nair, "NASA astronaut stands in as 'Mother Goose' for UBC study on high-flying geese," *CBC News* 03 Sept. 2019: 1-3. *Matrix of Symbols*

grabens: in the continuity of a rock formation, fractures caused by a shifting or dislodging of the earth's crust. The word is pronounced *grah*-bins. *Curiosity*

groat: a grain exclusive of the husk or hull. *The Embodied Robot*

Hades: in Greek mythology, the underworld of the dead. *Skein Winder*

Hadley Rille: In July 1971, during the Apollo 15 mission, Commander David Scott and "fellow moonwalker" James Irwin landed the lunar module Falcon about 0.5 kilometers from the planned landing site at Hadley-Apennine. *Hadley Rille* "is a lunar lava channel, and the Apennine Mountains form part of the rim of the Imbrium impact basin." See Andrew Chaikin, "While We Weren't Watching: Apollo's Scientific Exploration of the Moon," *The Planetary Report* May/June 1994: 2 <www.planetary.org/articles/while-we-werent-watching-apollo-science>. See also the historic Apollo surface photograph in Kerrod, *Space Walks* 40-41. *Quest*

halo-shaped: As a solar image, "the halo stands for the irradiation of supernatural light" (Chevalier and Gheerbrant, *The Penguin Dictionary of Symbols* 464-65). *Eternity's String*

hatch: here, a small door or opening, either the entrance or the exit of a spaceship. By contrast, the *airlock* contains *two* airtight doors, one for the entrance, the other for the exit. *Moonwalker*

Heaven's swain: here, either Ares, the adulterous lover of Aphrodite, or Robonaut 2, NASA's state-of-the-art humanoid, who "walks upright." *Posthuman*

Hecate: In ancient Greek mythology, the ambivalent *Hecate,* a lunar deity, is a "wild huntress" of the forest as well as "a real spook-goddess of night and phantoms [. . .]. As guardian of the gate of Hades and as the triple-bodied goddess of dogs, she is more or less identical with Cerberus. Thus, in bringing up Cerberus, Heracles [the sun-god that cremates himself] was really bringing the vanquished mother of death to the upper world" (C. G. Jung, *Symbols of Transformation,* trans. R. F. C. Hull [1956; Princeton: Princeton UP, 1990] 369). *Moonwalker*

He houses four cameras in his head; / For depth perception one more, infrared, / Mounted in his mouth: an excerpt from NASA's description of Robonaut 2, a dexterous humanoid robot designed for space travel: "Behind R2's visor are four visible light cameras—two to provide stereo vision for the robot and its operators, and two auxiliary [or backup] cameras. A fifth infrared camera is housed in the mouth area for depth perception" (*Robonaut 2: Fact Sheet* 2 <www.nasa.gov>). Accessed 10 Mar. 2022. *The Moon in Transition Raised to the Sun*

He journeys in the dark without an eye: Like the visionary artifex of line 24, Jesus sees not with His "outward" eyes, but rather—as Gerhard Dorn, the 16th-century philosophical alchemist, recommends—with "the eyes of the mind" or, better still, with "the eyes of the spirit" (Jung, *Psychology and Alchemy* 250-51, 269). *Wanderer*

He lists every coheir upon a chart; / Indwells all bodies; with his priestly art, / Maria the name inscribed upon his heart, / Divides Her axiom into each part: In *The Archetypes and the Collective Unconscious,* Jung explains the meaning of "the number 12," even as he clarifies the individuation process in its relation to astrological symbolism. Thus, "Twelve is four times three," a reconfiguration of the axiom of Maria Prophetissa, "that peculiar dilemma of three and four [. . .]. I would hazard that we have to do here with a *tetrameria* (as in Greek alchemy), a transformation process divided into four stages of three parts each, analogous to the twelve transformations of the zodiac and its division into four. As not infrequently happens, the number 12 would then have a not merely individual significance [as one's birth number, for instance], but a time-conditioned one too, since the present aeon of the Fishes is drawing to its end and is at the same time the twelfth house of the zodiac" (310). In short, as Jung also indicates in *Mysterium Coniunctionis,* since the soul "was imprinted with a horoscopic character at the time of its descent into birth," the journey of each mystic character through the planetary houses "boils down to becoming conscious" now of one's "godlikeness" (231). *Wanderer*

Helix from Heaven: i.e., the double helix, the physical structure of DNA, "the information molecule of all living systems: two linked strands that wind around each other" (Eric Green, "Double Helix," *National Human Genome Research Institute* 24 July 2024: 2 <genome.gov/genetics-glossary/Double-Helix-text>). *The Cradle of Life; Sphere*

He locomotes on an air-bearing sled: The speaker refers to The Exercise Countermeasures Laboratory (ECL) at NASA Glenn Research Center in Cleveland, Ohio, "a ground-based test bed which provides high-fidelity weightlessness," i.e., lunar and Martian "human-in-the-loop exercise simulations for developing exercise countermeasure devices, equipment, and exercise protocols for spaceflight." [In other words, "Exposure to microgravity induces physiological changes in astronauts," including bone loss and muscle atrophy.] Thus, "the test subjects are suspended in a supine orientation from a motorized system of bungees for weightlessness locomotion or exercise simulation, or at the appropriate pitch angle for whole-body partial gravity simulation." See Scott Graham and Timothy Reckart, "Exercise Countermeasures Lab," *NASA Glenn Research Center* 1-2 <www.grc.nasa.gov/space/human-research-program-advanced-exercise-concepts>. Last up-dated 13 Feb. 2024. *In the Outposts of Space*

Hephaestus: in Greek literature, the lame god who presides over fire, metals, and metallurgy. In Homer's *Odyssey,* he is also the husband of Aphrodite, the Goddess of Love. *The Cutting Edge of Haptics; The Embodied Robot; The Inner Lives of Robots; The Location of Earth; Magellan; Quest; The Quilted Multiverse; Saturn's Pebble; Scion; The Twin Paradox; Umbilicus*

Hephaestus' chain: See the note on *Hephaestus' strainer* given below. *Posthuman*

Hephaestus' strainer: Hephaestus, the cuckolded artisan of the gods, had "ensnared" Aphrodite, his wife, in a chain-link net, "when he caught her in the arms" of Ares, her lover (Michael Grant, *Myths of the Greeks and Romans* [Mentor-New American, 1964] 65). Here, *strainer* is, like the eye, not only a device for sifting, but also a curtailed form of "restrainer," since Hephaestus suppresses the dalliance of the compromised pair. *Quest*

He plants his boot; having sutured his seam, / Stands upon the mare, strapped to his dream: The speaker refers not only to the (physically) hyphenated astronaut, but also to the *lapis*—the living or animate stone—as the symbolic counterpart of the self. For a pertinent description of the NASA astronaut's spacesuit, see Kerry Mark Joels, Gregory P. Kennedy, and David Larkin, *The Space Shuttle Operator's Manual* (New York: Ballantine, 1982) 3.9: "the [Shuttle] spacesuit (more properly referred to as the extravehicular mobility unit, or EMU) [. . .] consists of three assemblies: the upper torso, the lower torso or trousers, and the portable life system. The upper torso and trousers separate into two units. A connecting ring around the waist joins them [. . .]." In other words, without that metal ring, physical self-division would result. Likewise, in the *lapis,* "the opposites are so to speak united," as Jung shows in *Aion,* "but with a visible seam or suture as in the symbol of the hermaphrodite." However, in the higher Adam, "the opposition is invisible" (247-48). In short, "The union of opposites in the stone [good, evil; consciousness, unconsciousness; male, female] is possible only when the adept has become One himself" (170). See also the note on *His partner yet sutured* given below. N.B.: The basic EMU was used on Space Shuttle flights from 1981-2002, with an improved version developed for International Space Station and Shuttle use in 1998 and beyond. *Moonwalker: The Twin Paradox*

He powers the world; the Paraclete stacked, / He indwells the foetus: Here, like heavenly data stored, arranged, or set up, the *Paraclete* is "the Holy Spirit [of the glorified Lord] given by God to those who are obedient to him" (Acts 5.32). See also Murray, *The Spirit of Christ* 13-14, and the note on *Paraclete* given below. *A Map of the Runner's Route*

Heracles: in Greek mythology, the Sun-hero [aka Hercules] "who submits to arduous labors and to the passion of self-cremation" and sublimation "culminating in divinity" (Jung, *Psychology and Alchemy* 381, 307n36). *Hyperspace*

He rides the stinger: On 16 November 1984, in order to capture *Westar VI,* a rogue communications satellite, the astronaut Dale Gardner, flying a Manned Maneuvering Unit and riding the *stinger,* "a spear-like probe, [. . .] jetted over to the spinning satellite, [. . .] inserted the stinger and locked onto the motor nozzle. With bursts of his MMU jets, he stopped the satellite [from] spinning and then jetted back to the waiting orbiter. There, the RMS [the Remote Manipulator System] arm reached out and grasped a grapple pin on the stinger to capture the satellite. The satellite was then lowered into the payload bay. But the final stowing of the satellite had to be done by hand, proving once again the need for the human touch in space maneuvers" (Kerrod, *Space Walks* 50). *The Embodied Robot*

herm: "a square pillar of stone topped by a bust or head, originally of Hermes" [the Greek god of revelation, the herald and messenger of the other gods] ("Herm" [n.], def.). *Scion*

Hermes: See the note on *Hermetic His hem* given below. *Posthuman; The Skin of the Rocket; Umbilicus*

Hermes' athanor: See Jung, *Alchemical Studies* B4: In the illustration, "To the right is the athanor (furnace) with the vessel in the centre, from which the lapis (hermaphrodite) will arise." *Magellan*

Hermes pends: Working outside his spacecraft, the NASA astronaut stands upon a foot restraint, NASA's portable platform. See also the pertinent note on *Hermetic His hem* given below. *Moonplant*

Hermes swallows His coheir like a stone: a variation on a cosmogonic Greek myth. See *Saturn fed / On Gaea's biped,* the note given below. The symbol of the Host in the Eucharistic feast is equally pertinent. *The Shape of Things to Come*

Hermetic His hem: The speaker underscores the androgyny of Christ, a union of opposites conceived, in the Christian religion, as "exclusively spiritual and symbolic" (Jung, *Psychology and Alchemy* 464). In alchemical literature, "Hermes or Mercurius possessed a double nature, being a chthonic god of revelation and also the spirit of quicksilver, for which reason he was represented as a hermaphrodite" (65). *Eternity's String; Saturn's Pebble; The Shape of Things to Come; The Skin of the Rocket; Umbilicus*

Hermetic redemption: the transformative renewal of life derived from the philosophy of Hermes Trismegistus, both the legendary first alchemist and emblematic magus. According to Jung, the redeemer-alchemists were "possessed by archetypes of a numinous nature" (*Psychology and Alchemy* 36), i.e., by "cosmogonic symbols" and their psychic effect (25). *Self-Recollection*

heron: a wading bird, an "anti-Satanic" creature, and therefore a symbol of Christ (Chevalier and Gheerbrant, *The Penguin Dictionary of Symbols* 503). *Driven*

Her skein: Clotho's ball of string. In Greek and Roman mythology, Clotho, one of three Fates, spins the thread of life that Lachesis measures and that Atropos cuts. *Hyperspace*

***He scaffolds the* rebis:** Scaffolding is "a process through which humans readily integrate incoming information with extant knowledge structures." In effect, "Features of abstract or less understood concepts are mapped onto existing and well understood concepts." Here, the hermaphroditic *rebis* is integrated with both the Spirit of Christ and "the consciousness-transcending fact [that] we call the self" (Jung, *Psychology and Alchemy* 202). For an updated view of the subject, see Lawrence E. Williams, Julia Y. Huang, and John A. Bargh, "The Scaffolded Mind: Higher mental processes are grounded in early experiences of the physical world," *The European Journal of Social Psychology*, 13 Nov. 2009: 39. *The Skin of the Rocket*

he sojourns like a moth: At this point, the astronaut, like the *moth*, becomes "a symbol of humanity in the chilly darkness, yearning for wings to take flight towards the heights of divine love" (Chevalier and Gheerbrant, *The Penguin Dictionary of Symbols* 676). *Driven*

He sought to be neither woman nor man, / But both these sexes: a description of the *rebis*, "The dual being born of the alchemical union of opposites" (masculine/feminine) and recognized "as a symbol of the self" (Jung, *Aion* 268). See also Rabbi Mark Sameth's illuminating essay "Is God Transgender?" in *The New York Times* 13 August 2016: A17: "the Hebrew Bible, when read in its original language, offers a highly elastic view of gender. And I do mean *highly* elastic: In Genesis 3:12, Eve is referred to as 'he.' In Genesis 9:21, after the flood, Noah repairs to 'her' tent. Genesis 24:16 refers to Rebecca as a 'young man.' And Genesis 1:27 refers to Adam as 'them.' [. . .] And there are many other, even more vivid examples: In Esther 2:17, Mordecai is pictured as nursing his niece Esther. In a similar way, in Isaiah 49:23, the future kings of Israel are prophesied to be 'nursing kings.' Why would the Bible do this? These aren't typos. [The answer is that] In the ancient world, well-expressed gender fluidity was the mark of a civilized person. Such a person was considered more 'godlike.' [. . .] Counter to everything [that] we grew up believing," the God of Israel "was understood by its earliest worshippers to be a dual-gendered deity." (Even Rabbi Daniel Ross Goodman, a respondent who subsequently disagreed with the latter thesis, maintained that "Positing a transgender God is the kind of bold, imaginative thinking that we sorely need in contemporary theology" ["Gender Identity in Olden Times: Interpreting the Torah," *The New York Times* 19 August 2016: A20].) *Rebis*

He waded in water: See John 3.22: "Jesus went into Judaea with his disciples, stayed there with them, and baptized. John too was baptizing at Aenon [EE-non], near to Salim [suh-LEEM], because water was plentiful in that region; and people were constantly coming for baptism." Later, in the same passage, John identifies himself as the forerunner of Christ: "'As he grows greater, I must grow less'" (3.30). *Eternity's String*

He walks like a bion: i.e., with the stiff, synchronized rhythms of an autonomous humanoid robot. The word is pronounced BYE-on. *Cosmologist*

He walks upright: The speaker refers to NASA's humanoid Robonaut and its automatic skill acquisition. See R. A. Peters, C. L. Campbell, W. J. Bluethmann, and E. Huber, "Robonaut task learning through teleoperation," a paper published in the *2003 IEEE International Conference on Robotics and Automation* (14-19 Sept. 2003). Significantly, as the authors indicate in their Abstract, the robot "was able to perform the [assigned] task autonomously with robot starting positions and object locations both similar to, and different from, the original trials." *Posthuman*

hieroglyph: "a picture or symbol representing a word, syllable, or sound, used by the ancient Egyptians and others, instead of alphabetical letters" ("Hieroglyphic" [n.], def. 1). *Magellan*

hierophant: either "a priest of a mystery cult," as in ancient Greece ("Hierophant" [n.], def. 1), or the archetypal God-man, "a person confidently expounding, explaining, or promoting something mysterious or obscure as though appointed to do so" (def. 2). *The Embodied Robot; Magellan; Matrix of Symbols; Moonplant; The Quilted Multiverse; Restoring Hubble's Vision; Ripples; Wanderer*

high-Ti basalt: rock located in the Descartes Highlands and returned from the Moon by the Apollo 16 mission. See A. L. Fagan and C. R. Neal, "A new lunar high-Ti basalt type defined from clasts [rock fragments] in Apollo 16 breccia [assorted cemented rock chips] 60639," *ScienceDirect* 12 Aug. 2015: 1 <www.sciencedirect.com>. *Quest*

hill of the raker: Golgotha, the skull-shaped *hill* in Jerusalem, the place of Christ's crucifixion. The *raker* is the skeleton with a scythe: Thanatos or Death, the Grim Reaper. *The Cutting Edge of Haptics*

His body wracked: The speaker refers to the Passion of Christ, a blend of narratives in the New Testament that includes the scourging, crowning with thorns, crucifixion, and the piercing of Jesus' side. For a succinct examination of the subject, see Richard Neitzel Holzapfel, "The Passion of Jesus Christ," BYU Religious Studies Center <rsc.byu.edu>. Accessed 26 Nov. 2023. *A Map of the Runner's Route*

His partner yet sutured: The speaker refers to the visible seam or portion of thread with which the opposites (light/darkness; consciousness/unconsciousness) are united, as in the symbol of the *rebis*. By contrast, in the higher Adam, "the opposition is invisible" (Jung, *Aion* 248). See also the note on *He plants his boot; having sutured his seam* given above. *Gravity and the Robonaut*

His roots in the air, his summits yet plumb: See the note on *mandrake* given below. *Clotho's Thrum*

His snow: the Mystical Body of Christ. See 1 Cor. 12.12-13: "For Christ is like a single body with its many limbs and organs, which, many as they are, together make up one body. For indeed we were all brought into one body by baptism, in the one Spirit, whether we are Jews or Greeks, whether slaves or free men, and that one Holy Spirit was poured out for all of us to drink." See also Jung, *Alchemical Studies* 214: In sundry Hermetic texts, the mercurial Spirit of the Lord "flies [purified] like solid white snow." *Driven*

his unit lists: the MMU (Manned Maneuvering Unit), a now-defunct propulsion device, couched here as a metonymy for the helmeted (and hence glass-encased) NASA astronaut, the wandering microcosm that *lists* or leans to the side. See the note on *Unfolds his unit* and also on *Unit, ghost, or probe* given below. *Ripples*

hoist; alight / That we may hitch a ride, without a bight, / Upon a foot restraint: a nod to the portable foot restraints that were "a standard crew aid on shuttle and International Space Station missions" and that NASA astronauts used as "a stable platform to stand on wherever they needed to work outside the spacecraft." Thus, whenever an astronaut serviced the Hubble Space Telescope, he placed mounting brackets for the foot restraints, strategically, around the shuttle payload bay and on the telescope to give him access to various worksites. "The spacewalker inserted the adjustable shaft into a bracket and then secured both booted feet under the toe bridges and into the heel clips." See "Foot Restraint, EVA, Portable, Hubble Space Telescope," *Smithsonian National Air and Space Museum* 3 <https://airandspace.si.edu>. Accessed 10 Mar. 2022. Incidentally, here, the playful *bight* is "a loop or slack part in a rope" ("Loop" [n.], def. 2). *The Moon in Transition Raised to the Sun*

hold: In the Space Shuttle Orbiter, the forward deck "contains the flight deck and crew quarters for the astronauts. During launch up to four astronauts may sit on the upper flight deck and up to four more on the middle crew quarters deck." Significantly, "at the aft end of the crew quarters deck is an air lock through which astronauts may enter the cargo bay when extravehicular activities are necessary." *Umbilicus*

the hole with teeth: a black hole, "a compressed star with a reputation for rapacity, since objects of any composition whatsoever that get too close—closer than what has been termed the black hole's event horizon—[. . .] cannot escape from its gravitational grip" (Brian Greene, *The Elegant Universe: Superstrings, Hidden Dimensions, and the Quest for the Ultimate Theory* 79). *Driven; Hyperspace*

holon: a whole embedded in larger wholes; hence, an entity—whether an atom or a universe—that is both a whole and a part. Arthur Koestler coined the term in *The Ghost in the Machine* (1967; New York: Arkana-Penguin, 1990) 48. *Colossus; The Embodied Robot; Erasure; Finger's Grain; Link; A Map of the Runner's Route; Rebis*

Honey: According to the alchemists, "The elixir of honey preserves and cleanses the human body from all imperfections, both within and without" (Jung, *Mysterium Coniunctionis* 479n81). *Restoring Hubble's Vision*

Horeb: a cloud-covered site—usually identified with Mount Sinai—where Moses received the law from God. See Exod. 24.12: "The Lord said to Moses, 'Come up to me on the mountain, stay there and let me give you the tablets of stone, the law and the commandment, which I have written down that you may teach them.'" *Ripples*

the Horus-child: the falcon-headed Egyptian sky-god, the son of Isis and Osiris. His right eye represented the sun; his left eye, the moon. "His legendary battle with Set, whom he cut to pieces but who tore out one of his eyes [his moon-eye], is an example of the struggle [between] light and darkness [. . .]" (Chevalier and Gheerbrant, *The Penguin Dictionary of Symbols* 528). *Clotho's Thrum*

the Host in the mill: In *How to Know Higher Worlds,* trans. Christopher Bamford (1961; New York: Anthroposophic P, 1994), Rudolph Steiner asserts that the supreme task of humankind "is to harvest from the mortal world fruits for the immortal" (199). See also *Psychology and Alchemy* 306, where Jung describes a "myth-picture" (fig. 158) titled "Mill of the Host": "The Word, in the form of scrolls, is poured into a mill by the four evangelists, to reappear as the Infant Christ in the chalice" (307). The illustration punctuates a theme germane both to Christianity and to alchemy—that "redemption is a *work*" (306). *The Mill of the Host*

Host in the vessel, first-born in the beam: See John 8.12: "Once again Jesus addressed the people: 'I am the light of the world. No follower of mine shall wander in the dark; he shall have the light of life.'" See also Col. 1.15: "He is the image of the invisible God, born before all created things." The note on *the Host in the Mill* given above is equally pertinent. *Wanderer*

the Host of herds: both a pun and a twofold allusion, not only to Christ and His worshippers, but also to the Eucharistic bread and its communicants. *Pioneer*

host of shards honed: a heap of either glass or rock fragments both sharpened and polished. In alchemy, oftentimes, the desired goal—among vague and various conceptions—is either "the philosopher's stone" or "the golden glass" (Jung, *Psychology and Alchemy* 232). For a separate yet not unrelated reading of this phrase, see Jung, *The Archetypes and the Collective Unconscious* 328n115, where, "In consequence of the Fall, the host of shards irrupted into Adam's body, its outer layers being more infected than the inner ones." However, according to a Christian interpretation of the *Kabbala Denudata* from the 17th century, "The 'Anima Christi' fought and finally destroyed the shards, which signify matter." *Clotho's Thrum*

hub: here, either the Sun, which the planet Earth orbits once a year, or the central portion of the Milky Way Galaxy, around which our entire solar system revolves once every 225 million years. For an alternate reading of this term, see the note on *I stepped from its hub, departed its hold* given below. *Umbilicus*

Hubble: i.e., the *Hubble* Space Telescope, named after Edwin Powell *Hubble* (1889-1953), an American astronomer who recognized, along with other astronauts, that the universe is expanding. Launched on the Space Shuttle *Discovery* on 24 April 1990, *Hubble,* the observatory, "is the first major optical telescope to be placed in space, the ultimate mountaintop. [. . .] Scientists have used Hubble to observe the most distant stars and galaxies as well as the planets in our solar system." See Rob Garner, "About the Hubble Space Telescope," *NASA* 2 <www.nasa.gov>. Last updated on 12 December 2017. [NB: NASA launched the James Webb Space Telescope, its successor to the *Hubble,* on 25 December 2021.] *Restoring Hubble's Vision*

Hunter-gatherer: Until around 11,000 to 12,000 years ago, our nomadic ancestors emphasized both the hunting of animals and the gathering of wild vegetation for food. *Wanderer*

Hymen's own species: In Greek myth, Hymen is "the God of the Wedding Feast" (Hamilton, *Mythology* 36), an attendant of the Eros, the son of Aphrodite, that all men serve. *The Embodied Robot; Posthuman*

Hypercube: a cube in four dimensions; unraveled, it becomes a three-dimensional, "crosslike tesseract" (Michio Kaku, *Hyperspace* [New York: Oxford UP, 1994] 70-71). *Finger's Grain*

hyperspace: "higher-dimensional space"—according to superstring theory, "the three dimensions of space (length, width, and breadth) and one of time [. . .] extended by six or more spatial dimensions" (Kaku, *Hyperspace* vii-viii). *Gravity and the Robonaut; Hyperspace; Umbilicus*

hyphenate: a person, place, or thing of mixed identity. *A Map of the Runner's Route*

I affirm His Spirit: i.e., "the [indwelling] Spirit of the Father of Jesus Christ" (Murray, *The Spirit of Christ* 5). *A Map of the Runner's Route*

I climb the helix: See the note on *Helix from Heaven* given above. *Sphere*

I hauled in my dew-cart aerial lead: i.e., the *lead* of the air, in alchemy the spirit of life that—"nourished by the stars"—the metallic earth "hatches" in its womb (Jung, *Psychology and Alchemy* 342). *Restoring Hubble's Vision*

incubate its stray: here, "to cause [the wandering human animal] to develop or take form, as by thought or planning" ("Incubate" [vt.], def. 3). *Wanderer*

Index the Secret: Here, the "Scions of Eden" (l. 21) must identify the prayer said just before the Preface of the Mass. *Finger's Grain*

I near the fire: In this stanza, "The fire is like unto Christ, an *imago Christi*" (Jung, *Psychology and Alchemy* 353). *Self-Recollection*

An infinite bubble and then the Bang: according to contemporary cosmologists and astrophysicists, "the infinite bubbling potential from which [. . .] the universe arose before the Big Bang" (Margaret Wertheim, "God Is Also a Cosmologist," *The New York Times* 8 June 1997: 2 <www.nytimes.com/1997/06/08/weekinreview/god-is-also-a-cosmologist>. *Cosmologist*

In His crimson splendor, Mars—not the beast—: not the red planet inhospitable to life, but the robust Greek God of War instead. For further elaboration, see the note on *Chain-link that twines the pair* given above. *Curiosity*

In Man's hand the compass, in Woman's the square: In typical alchemical illustrations, the hermaphroditic *Rebis* holds two objects. On the left side, the male holds the architect's *compass,* which represents the heavenly circle; on the right side, the female holds a carpenter's earthly *square,* an instrument used to lay out or test quadrilateral space. In other words, here, the Male and the Female are united as One in alchemy's royal marriage—"the mingling of the subtle with the dense" (Jung, *Aion* 167n50)—like inward and outward work. See the note on *The Crowned Hermaphrodite* and also on *the Host in the mill* given above. *The Mill of the Host*

In my bubble I can swim like a fish: Cf. Kitzinger and Nilsson, *Being Born,* where the embryonic "ball of cells grew and grew till it looked like a shimmering, silvery blackberry" (15) and where, weeks later, the warm foetus swam fishlike "in a bubble of water" (30). *A Map of the Runner's Route*

In my heart a hill: i.e., Golgotha, the Place of the Skull, where Jesus was crucified (Mark 19.17-18). *Self-Recollection*

in Pictor amid M-type worlds / A rogue with twin mini-Neptunes unfurls: a cosmic snapshot. "In 2019, NASA's Transiting Exoplanet Survey Satellite (TESS) discovered a super-earth and two mini-Neptunes orbiting a faint, cool star about 73 light-years away in the southern constellation of Pictor. The M-type dwarf star is about 40% smaller than the Sun in both size and mass, and it has a surface temperature about one-third cooler than the Sun's." See Pat Brennan, Kristen Walholt, and Travis Schirner, "NASA Exoplanet Exploration – Planets Beyond our Solar System": 2 <https://exoplanets.nasa.gov>. Updated 13 Apr. 2022. *Exoplanets*

Instantiate: "to represent by a concrete example" ("Instantiate" [vt.], def.). *Driven*

In the fraction of a second I pause, / Feel His Presence, then intuit His cause— / Near to the fire, I contemplate His laws: The self-transforming speaker identifies three of the four functions of consciousness: Feeling, Intuiting, and Thinking—Self-sensing is implicit—even as he channels or converts the instinctual activities of those functions into analogues of salvation. The entire venture—a map of the Christian runner's route—is meant to validate Jung's assertion in *The Archetypes and the Collective Unconscious* that, although consciousness can never supersede the totality of the psyche—indeed, consciousness can exist only "through the [human percipient's] continual recognition of the unconscious" (96)—"Every advance, even the smallest, along this path of conscious realization adds that much to the world" (96). *A Map of the Runner's Route*

Into the mind Ge's mythologem let: / Cognition's offspring, His astronaut met / Like the nascent Self, transcendental yet: In *Aion,* Jung reminds us that the *psychological* self "is completely outside the personal sphere, and appears, if at all, only as a religious mythologem" (62-63). In fact, like other "empirical symbols of totality" (31), the Christ-image "fully corresponds to this situation: Christ is the perfect man who is crucified. One could hardly think of a truer picture of the goal of ethical endeavour. At any rate the transcendental idea of the self that serves psychology as a working hypothesis can never match that image because, although it is a symbol, it lacks the character of a revelatory historical event" (69). *Eternity's String*

Into the noise of the fireball we peer: i.e., into cosmogony's hum—the static due to "the radiation left over from the fireball that filled the Universe at the beginning of its existence" (Jastrow, *God and the Astronomers* 20-21). *Magellan*

I nudged a cloud once: The speaker recalls the simultaneous occurrence of a thought—the *cloud* plume happening in his mind—with the corkscrew towering in the sky, even as, during one late summer afternoon on a college campus, distracted, he crossed an empty street. In fact, this is the type of "absolute synchronism of psychic and physical events" that Gottfried Wilhelm von Leibniz (1646-1716) and Arthur Schopenhauer (1788-1860) had explored and that, later, C. G. Jung had examined as both "a special instance of general acausal orderedness" and a meaningful coincidence—an act of *"creation in time"*—in *Synchronicity: An Acausal Connecting Principle,* trans. R. F. C. Hull (Princeton: Princeton UP, 1973) 100-01. *Copy*

I process the cosmos, a gram of salt: The speaker brackets the "arcane substance" hidden in the primordial chaos with Christ, "the salt of wisdom [. . .] given at baptism" (Jung, *Mysterium Coniunctionis* 241). *Erasure*

I range beyond Neptune: Among planets a gas giant, *Neptune*—"which is 35 times farther from the Sun than Earth is"—was observed by Voyager 2, "almost continuously," from June to October, 1989. See Steve Fimbres and Luis Espinoza, "Neptune Approach," *Voyager* n.d: 1-2 <voyager.jpl.nasa.gov/mission/science>. Accessed 08/14/24. *The Location of Earth*

I reach in my hour to birth like a bride: The speaker refers to the *birth* of the self, "not the empirical man, but rather the indescribable totality of the psychic or spiritual man, who cannot be described because he is compounded of consciousness as well as of the indeterminable extent of the unconscious" (Jung, *The Archetypes and the Collective Unconscious* 308.) See the note on *A joyful giant* given below and also 2 Cor. 11.2: "I am jealous for you, with a divine jealousy; for I betrothed you to Christ, thinking to present you as a chaste virgin to her true and only husband." *Pioneer*

I rocket to the moon in Sol's disguise: the NASA astronaut compared to the ancient Roman sun-god. *Copy*

I spin like a wheel: See Chevalier and Gheerbrant, *The Penguin Dictionary of Symbols:* In the majority of cultures, the wheel "is a solar symbol" (1099), even as the Sun itself is either a god or "a manifestation of the godhead" (945). *The Location of Earth*

I stand to the North; that light may enter, / A wayfarer still, I search the center / Round as an eye: See Chevalier and Gheerbrant, *The Penguin Dictionary of Symbols* 1112-13: "In *Freemasonry,* the [diagrammatic] Tracing Boards of the Apprentice and Fellowcraft Mason depict three windows, covered with gratings, like the windows of the Temple of Jerusalem described in 1 Kings 6:4. These three windows are said to correspond to east, south and west, the three 'stations' of the Sun. No window corresponds to the north, through which the Sun does not pass. This is to allow light to be received at these three stages and perhaps under three different modalities." Significantly, "The Apprentice stands to the north, so as to receive the greatest intensity of light through the southern window." The authors add that "In so far as it opens to air and light, the window symbolizes receptivity. If the window is round, the receptivity is the same as the eye's and that of consciousness. If it is square, it is terrestrial receptivity, in contrast with the gifts of Heaven." *The Mill of the Host*

I stepped from its hub, departed its hold, / [. . .] Contained the cosmos, like a Scripture scrolled: Here, the astronaut steps from his moonship in a "space-time landscape [that] unfolds like a scroll with all moments and events co-existing within it, though we view these sequentially, one by one, as the scroll unfolds" (Shalini Asha Bhaloo, *Oneness: How to Live with Joyous Expansion, Ease, and Lightness* [Bloomington: Balboa P, 2012] 112). See also Jason Lisle, "Worlds of Creation," *Biblical Science Institute* 10 Apr. 2020: 1: ". . . the Earth is uniquely designed for life (Isaiah 45:18). This makes it quite different from any known world. And while it may not be the center of the physical universe, the Earth is certainly critical to God's plan of redemption" (1). NB: The definition of *hold* is given above. *Umbilicus*

its mien like a maw: its look or appearance compared to the jaws of a voracious animal—here, of the mythical dragon. *Sphere*

Its sticky silk blown—/ Zigzag sunburst: The speaker refers to the Silver Argiope spider web, with crossed zigzag bands like the spreading rays of the sun. See Herbert W. Levi and Lorna R. Levi, *A Guide to Spiders and Their Kin* (New York: Golden-Western, 1968) 68-69. *Erasure*

I weave the skein of my life into form— / Create found shapes: here, out of chaos, a seed of cosmic unity, as Chevalier and Gheerbrant calculate in *The Penguin Dictionary of Symbols* 1093: "Cloth, THREAD, loom, SPINDLE and DISTAFF, whatever is used in spinning and weaving, all these are so many symbols of futurity. They are used to denote all that rules or intervenes in our fate. The Moon 'weaves' destiny and the spider, spinning its web, is an image of our fate. The Fates themselves were spinsters, weaving the threads of destiny, and they were Moon-deities, too. To weave is to create fresh shapes." See also Jung, *Psychology and Alchemy* 25: "every act of dawning consciousness is a creative act, and it is from this psychological experience that all our cosmogonic symbols are derived." *The Mill of the Host*

I will dwell in them and thus walk with them: Cf. Murray, The *Spirit of Christ* 42-43: "The baptism of the Spirit is the endowment with power to fill us with boldness and give [us] the victory over the world and every enemy. It is the fulfillment of what God meant in His promise: 'I will dwell in them, and walk in them' [2 Cor. 6.16]." In effect, each believer becomes the *temple* of God. See also the note on *Wakened from the dead, I will walk with them,* an alternate version of this line given below. *Eternity's String*

Jarosite: a hydrated mineral on the Red Planet Mars. *Murphy's Law on Mars*

J-hook: a cable support made of galvanized steel or plastic polymers. *The Embodied Robot*

jinn: in popular usage, a single supernatural being that can assume either human or animal form. *The Teleoperator's Cue*

Joins his torsos with a connecting ring: Ready to connect the upper and lower assemblies of his spacesuit [the extravehicular mobility unit, or the Shuttle's EMU], the NASA astronaut feels and hears a series of faint clicks as the ring joints catch (Kerry Mark Joels, Gregory P. Kennedy, and David Larkin, *The Space Shuttle Operator's Manual* (New York: Ballantine, 1982) 3.10-3.11. *Hyperspace*

A joyful giant: In this stanza, the speaker views Christ as both the mercurial "Giant of twofold substance" (Jung, *Alchemical Studies* 292-93nn4-5) and the solar Savior of Psalm 19.5, "who comes out like a bridegroom from his wedding canopy, / rejoicing like a strong man to run his race." *Wanderer*

Keep or steeple: either "a stronghold, fort, [or] castle" ("Keep" [n.], def. 2b), or "a church tower with a spire" ("Steeple" [n.], def. 2). *The Mill of the Host*

Ken: a male doll—the counterpart to Barbie—introduced by Mattel, an American toy company, in 1959. *The Embodied Robot*

ken: "mental perception; range of knowledge; [or] understanding" ("Ken" [n.], def. 2). *The Twin Paradox*

Kepler's eye: The speaker affirms the vision of Johannes Kepler (1571-1630), a German astronomer and mathematician. *Habitat*

Kepler's super-earth: "a planet a little more than one and a half times as big in radius as Earth. Known as Kepler 452b, it circles a sunlike star in an orbit that takes 385 days, just slightly longer than our own year, putting it firmly in the 'Goldilocks' habitable zone where the temperatures are lukewarm and suitable for liquid water on the surface—if it has a surface. [. . .] The star that lights this planet's sky is about 1.5 billion years older than our sun and 20 percent more luminous, which has implications for the prospects of life." See Dennis Overbye, "NASA Says Data Reveals an Earth-Like Planet, Kepler 452b," *The New York Times* 23 July 2015: 1 <www.nytimes.com/2015/07/24/science/space/kepler-data>. *Centauri Dreams*

Kevlar: a brand name for a heat-resistant, synthetic fiber used in making the outer layer of the Shuttle spacesuit. *Copy*

kite: a predatory bird of the hawk family, "with long, pointed wings and, usually, a forked tail" ("Kite" [n.], def. 1). *Skein Winder*

the Kuiper [KYE-per] ***Belt:*** a region of the solar system beyond the orbit of Neptune. The first spacecraft to enter the *Kuiper Belt* region was NASA's Pioneer 10 spacecraft in 1983. *The Location of Earth*

The labyrinth of webs that Clotho purled: In Greek and Roman mythology, *Clotho,* one of three Fates, spins the thread of life that Lachesis measures and that Atropos cuts. Here, in order to produce a ribbed effect, *Clotho* apparently inverts her stitches with an elastic thread. *Hyperspace*

Laith: a gender-neutral given name of Scottish origin. *Cosmologist*

lapis: in alchemy, the philosophers' stone taken as a symbol of the unified self, i.e., "of the inner Christ, of God in man" (Jung, *Alchemical Studies* 96). *Colossus*

lead: In alchemy, *lead* is, like Adam, an hermaphroditic "transformative substance" (Jung, *Mysterium Coniunctionis* 382). *Restoring Hubble's Vision*

Leprous: an alchemical epithet—either impure, unclean, contaminated, or corrupt, like "metals, oxides, and salts" (Jung, *Alchemical Studies* 290n6). *The Twin Paradox*

Lichen, archaeon: Here, *Lichen* refers to "any of various small plants composed of a particular fungus and a particular alga [seaweeds or pond scum] growing in an intimate symbiotic association and forming a dual plant, commonly adhering in colored patches or sponge-like branches to rock, wood, [or] soil" ("Lichen" [n.], def. 1). Equally fascinating is the *archaeon,* a microorganism that adapts to, and survives in, extreme environments. *The Cradle of Life*

light smith: here, the moonchild as the medium of illumination that makes insight possible. *The Location of Earth*

Like a bean: a prenatal image. See Kitzinger and Nilsson, *Being Born* 22: In the womb, "You didn't look much like a baby yet—more like a sprouting bean." *A Map of the Runner's Route*

Like a bubble that shimmers in its pan: Cf. Kitzinger and Nilsson, *Being Born* 30, where the embryonic "ball of cells grew and grew till it looked like a shimmering, silvery blackberry" (15) and where, weeks later, the warm foetus swam fishlike "in a bubble of water." *Rebis*

like a thread, projected from a cam: in camera mount and tripod use, the screw *thread* that secures the camera onto the mount. Usually a male (external) *thread* functions on the mount and a matching female (internal) *thread* on the camera or lens. *The Orphan in His Pram*

Like circle and triangle bound to the quad: the Christian sojourner framed as a circumscribed human cross. Cf. Jung, *The Archetypes and the Collective Unconscious* 382: "It is evident that individuation, or becoming whole, is neither a *summum bonum* nor a *summum desideratum,* but the painful experience of the union of opposites. That is the real meaning of the cross in the circle [. . .]." *Centauri Dreams*

Like fire that in the churn the lizard licks: In Hermetic texts, the *lizard* is a symbol of heavenly transformation—"The Mercurial spirit of the *prima materia,* in the shape of a salamander, frolicking in the fire" (Jung, *Psychology and Alchemy* 276, fig. 138). See also Chevalier and Gheerbrant, *The Penguin Dictionary of Symbols* 614, where the islanders of the Torres Straits "believe that it was a long-necked lizard which brought fire to [hu]mankind." *Ripples*

Like Martian episodes from Venus' fane: The speaker recalls alchemical procedures that represent cyclical death and renewal. Thus, at the end of the Regimen of Venus, the color "changes into a livid purple, whereupon the philosophical tree will blossom. Then follows the regimen of Mars," during which the soaring colors of the rainbow and of the peacock appear (Jung, *Mysterium Coniunctionis* 288-89). *Finger's Grain*

Like spokes of the wheel that all life pursues: in the tenth major Arcanum of the TAROT, the Wheel of Fortune, i.e., "a solar symbol, the wheel of life and death following on one another's heels throughout the cosmos and, at a human level, perpetual mutability and eternal homecoming. 'Human life runs changeably onwards like the spokes of a chariot-wheel,' Anacreon [the ancient Greek poet] wrote." Chevalier and Gheerbrant add that "The wheel falls into the general category of emanation and return, symbols which give expression to the development of the universe and of the individual" (*The Penguin Dictionary of Symbols* 1103-04). *The Mill of the Host*

Like the Spirit indwelt, or His temple prized: / Ge's immortal percept actualized: Here, the *percept* or "impression received by the mind through the senses" ("Percept" [n.], def.) underscores the relationship between the believer and the Spirit of the Glorified Jesus. Thus, in *The Spirit of Christ,* Murray affirms that each believer "must learn to know that there is a holiest of all in that temple which he himself is; the secret place of the most high within us must become the central truth in our temple worship" (160). See also Jung, *Alchemical Studies* 338, where Jung observes that, "when the man's femininity, the anima, or the woman's masculinity, the animus, is not differentiated enough to be integrated with consciousness, [. . .] the self is only potentially present as an intuition but is not yet actualized." *Cosmologist*

The lotus-seat: "The Son of God, God made manifest, dwells in the flower"—the Buddha in the lotus, Christ in the rose (Jung, *Psychology and Alchemy* 107-08). *Clotho's Thrum*

magus: "a sorcerer or [an] astrologer" ("Magus" [n.], def. 2)—here, either the ever-gestating NASA astronaut or "the inner, eternal man [hidden] in the shell of the outer, mortal man" (Jung, *Alchemical Studies* 150), the maker of this poem. *Sphere; The Shape of Things to Come*

mandrake: the root of the mandragora, a medicinal plant, formerly thought to possess occult powers because of its supposed resemblance to the human body—specifically, to a man standing upside down. In *Alchemical Studies*, Jung notes that "The idea that man is an inverted tree seems to have been current in the Middle Ages. [. . .] In Hindu literature the tree grows from above downwards, whereas in alchemy (at least according to the pictures) it grows from below upwards." However, "In East and West alike, the tree symbolizes a living process as well as a process of enlightenment" (312-14)—in fine, the work of both "[moral] transformation and [spiritual] renewal" (317). See also *Carrying the Fire: An Astronaut's Journey* (1974; New York: Ballantine-Random, 1975) 371, where Michael Collins describes his own "inverted tree" scene from the Apollo 11 expedition: "The world outside my window is breathtaking; in the three short years since Gemini 10, I have forgotten how beautiful it is, as clouds and sea slide majestically and silently by. We are [lying in individual couches] 'upside down,' in that our heads are pointed down toward the earth and our feet toward the black sky, and this is the position in which we will remain for the next two and a half hours in earth orbit, as we prepare ourselves and our machine for the next big step, the translunar injection burn which will propel us toward the moon. The reason for the heads-down attitude is to allow the sextant, in the belly of the C[ommand] M[odule], to point up at the stars, for one of the most important things I must do is [to] take a couple of star sightings to make sure that our guidance and navigation equipment is working properly before we decide to take the plunge and leave our safe earth orbit." *Erasure; Pioneer*

Maneuver my unit: i.e., the MMU (Manned Maneuvering Unit), a now-defunct propulsion device, couched here as a metonymy for the helmeted (and hence glass-encased) NASA astronaut. The term evokes the image of the astronaut as a wandering microcosm. See also the note on *My unit manned* given below. *The Twin Paradox*

Manifestation of the God that girds: Christ portrayed as both Savior and warrior King. See John 3.17: "It was not to judge the world that God sent His Son into the world, but that through him the world might be saved," and Rev. 19.11: "Then I saw heaven wide open, and there before me was a white horse; and its rider's name was Faithful and True, for he is just in judgement and just in war." *Pioneer*

manna: the food given by God to the Israelites during the exodus from Egypt: "Israel called the food manna; it was white, like coriander seed, and it tasted like a wafer made with honey" (Exod. 16.31). *Posthuman*

A Map of the Runner's Route: In the title poem, and throughout this book, even as he performs the four functions of consciousness—Sensing, Intuiting, Feeling, and Thinking—the speaker converts the instinctual energy of those activities into analogues of salvation. The entire venture—a veritable map of the runner's route—is meant to validate Jung's assertion in *The Archetypes and the Collective Unconscious* that, although consciousness can never supersede the totality of the psyche—indeed, consciousness can exist only "through [the human percipient's] continual recognition of the unconscious" (96)—"Every advance, even the smallest along the path of conscious realization, adds that much to the world" (97). See also 1 Tim. 6.12, a pertinent passage: "Run the great race of faith and take hold of eternal life." *A Map of the Runner's Route*

mare: a dark plain on the Earth's moon. The word is pronounced MAH-ray. *Clotho's Thrum; Colossus; The Inner Lives of Robots; Moonwalker; Rebis*

Maria the name inscribed upon his heart: the alchemist of Gnostic tradition, the legendary "Prophetissa" and reputed "sister of Moses" (Jung, *Psychology and Alchemy* 401n169). See the note on *axiom* given above. *Wanderer*

The marriage of the subtile with the dense: "the physical and the psychic [. . .] blended in an indissoluble unity" (Jung, *Psychology and Alchemy* 279). See the clarifying note on *matter that sang: / Ge's own mythologem* given below. *Centauri Dreams*

Matter is not static: quantum its home: According to the Everett-DeWitt many-universes interpretation of *quantum* theory, our local world "is continually splitting into countless near copies of itself. [. . .] In addition to this ceaseless replication, our own bodies are part of the world, and they too are split and split again. Not only our bodies, but our brains and, presumably, our consciousness [are] being repeatedly multiplied, each copy becoming a thinking, feeling human being inhabiting another universe much like the one we see around us" (Davies, *Other Worlds* 136-37). See also the note on *quantum* given below. *Umbilicus*

matter that sang: / Ge's own mythologem: i.e., Christ, in the poem, "An animate substance" (l. 1), "'the [philosophic] stone that is no stone, nor of the nature of stone'" (Jung, *Alchemical Studies* 292). See also 288-89, where the speaker echoes Jung's defense of "a psychology that demonstrates the necessity of psychic premises." Thus, "Whereas the scientific attitude seeks, on the basis of careful empiricism, to explain nature in her own terms, Hermetic philosophy had for its goal an explanation that included the psyche in a total description of nature." In other words, the Hermetic philosopher "was not yet so dominated by the object that he could ignore the palpable presence of psychic premises in the form of eternal ideas [the archetypes] which he felt to be real. The empirical nominalist, on the other hand, already had the modern attitude toward the psyche, namely, that it had to be eliminated as something 'subjective.' His hope was to be able to produce a picture of the world that was entirely independent of the observer." Nevertheless, "This hope has been fulfilled only in part, as the findings of modern physics show: the observer cannot be finally eliminated, which means that the psychic premises remain operative." *Cosmologist*

Mechatronic polyglot: a robotic multilinguist, the "Instrumented cyborg" of line 8. *Link*

Melissa preferred: not only the Greek nymph who taught the use of honey and was transformed thereafter into a beautiful bee (Louis Charbonneau-Lassay, *The Bestiary of Christ*, trans. D. M. Dooling [1940; New York: Arkana-Penguin, 1992] 320-21), but also, in alchemy, an arcanum that Paracelsus had "singled out for special honour because in ancient medicine it was considered to be a means of inducing happiness, and was used as a remedy for melancholia and for purging the body [. . .]" (Jung, *Alchemical Studies* 153). *Self-Recollection*

Melt from the magma: In geology, *magma* is molten and semi-molten rock found deep in the earth, a mixture that includes the melt, its hot liquid base. *Erasure*

The membrane in the sea that starfish sow: Because it can regenerate its lost limbs, the *starfish* symbolizes both the power of *self*-renewal and the resilience of life. See the picture of "the under or oral surface of a starfish" in "Starfish (Asteroids)," *Cronodon BioTech* [n.d.]: 2 <https://cronodon.com .html>. *Pioneer*

meme: "a concept or behavior that spreads [like the transmission of genes] from person to person. Examples of memes include beliefs, fashions, stories, and phrases" typically dispersed "within local cultures or social groups" or through the Internet ("Meme," *TechTerms* 28 Nov. 2011 <www.techterms.com>). The popular term was coined in 1976 by the evolutionary biologist Richard Dawkins in *The Selfish Gene*. *The Inner Lives of Robots*

Metallic his shield: The speaker refers to "a [foldable] metallic space fabric made of interlocking stainless steel squares. It looks like chain mail, but unlike the ancient armor, NASA's fabric isn't welded together. Instead, a 3-D printer extrudes stainless steel as a continuous sheet of material with different properties on each side. From the front of the fabric, rows of shiny, flat squares can reflect heat and light. On the back, a series of interlocking loops help the fabric absorb heat. Together, the single piece of material acts like a super-strong shield, protecting astronauts and spacecrafts from outer orbit's deadly obstacles" (Liz Stinson, "NASA's Wild Fabric Is Basically Chain Mail From the Future," WIRED 16 June 2017: 2 <www.wired.com/story/nasa-fabric-chain-mail-from-the-future>). *Pioneer*

Metallic the Tree that harbors the key: in alchemy, not only the mystical world-tree, "whose shining fruits are the stars" (Jung, *Alchemical Studies* 310), but also the inverted tree, i.e., "man as a tree standing upside down"—both an "earthly" and a "heavenly" plant (312). *Saturn's Pebble*

Methane on Titan: "Titan's surface and atmosphere have an active hydrological cycle, though with a condensable liquid other than water." In fact, "lakes are filled through methane rainfall or interact with a subsurface layer saturated with liquid methane." See *"ESA – Titan* *has liquid lakes!"* The European Space Agency 03/01/2007: 3 <europa.nasa.gov>. *The Cradle of Life*

The midpoint of the center: i.e., fire, because "fire is active, spiritual, emotional, close to consciousness, whereas water is passive, material, cool, and of the nature of the unconscious." However, "Both are necessary," since the goal of alchemy "is concerned with the union of opposites" (Jung, *Alchemical Studies* 151n78). Elsewhere, Jung remarks that fire is "an internal component of the deity" (209). *Wanderer*

mime: a silent or mute impersonator—here, an imitator of Christian piety. *Eternity's String*

Möbius' (MER-be-us) run: one of the many strange topologies of hyperspace—a continuous, one-sided geometric surface "created by twisting a strip of paper 180 degrees and then gluing the ends together." In effect, "outside and inside are identical" (Kaku, *Hyperspace* 60-61). The "Möbius strip" is named after its deviser, the nineteenth-century German mathematician A. F. Möbius. *The Inner Lives of Robots; The Moon in Transition Raised to the Sun; Murphy's Law on Mars*

Möbius' strand: an infinite loop, here a metaphor for the universe. See the note on *Möbius' run* given above. *The Moon in Transition Raised to the Sun; Murphy's Law on Mars; Self-Recollection: The Teleoperator's Cue*

moil: "confusion; turmoil" ("Moil" [n.], def. 2). *Link*

Molecular swirls that cyborgs yet breach: breakthrough human brain spirals that travel across the cortex, "engage in intricate interactions" and play "a crucial role in organizing the brain's complex activities." See Philip Ritchie, "Scientists discover spiral-shaped signals that organize brain activity" (*The University of Sydney News,* 16 June 2023: 1 <www.sydney.edu.au/news-opinion/news/2023/06/16>). *Murphy's Law on Mars*

Monad: not only the indivisible point—"the jot of the iota"—viewed as a Gnostic emblem of the totalistic man or woman (Jung, *Aion* 218), but also a basic unit of matter—a microcosm—that, according to the German philosopher and mathematician Gottfried Wilhelm von Leibnitz (1646-1716), mirrors the universe. *Erasure; The Location of Earth; Moonwalker; Rebis; Saturn's Pebble; The Shape of Things to Come*

moonchild: "a prefiguration of the [archetypal] self"—in alchemy, "the spagyric embryo conceived by the sun in [the] womb and belly" of the moon (Jung, *Mysterium Coniunctionis* 175-76). *The Quilted Multiverse*

The moon in transition raised to the sun: a symbolic picture of spiritual androgyny and the totalistic self. See Jung, *Psychology and Alchemy* 231-32: "the first main goal" of the alchemical process is the *albedo,* "highly prized by many alchemists as if it were the ultimate goal. It is the silver or moon condition, which still has to be raised to the sun condition. The *albedo* is, so to speak, the daybreak, but not till the *rubedo* is it sunrise." In effect, "The red and white are King and Queen, who may also celebrate their 'chymical wedding' at this stage" of the *opus,* i.e., the royal marriage of opposites that always occurs—not only in the emblematic

Christ, the divine "bridegroom" (389), but also in His born-again believers—"outside the natural context" (464-65). See also 231, fig. 116: "Crowned hermaphrodite representing the union of king and queen, [standing] between the sun and moon trees." *The Moon in Transition Raised to the Sun*

moonplant: In alchemy, "the moon itself is a plant" (Jung, *Mysterium Coniunctionis* 132). Thus, in the alchemical pictures, sometimes the prototype of the tree of paradise is "hung not with apples but with sun-and-moon fruit" (Jung, *Alchemical Studies* 303). *Colossus; Moonplant*

moth: "the moth is the constant symbol of the soul seeking the godhead and consumed by a mystical love" (Chevalier and Gheerbrant, *The Penguin Dictionary of Symbols* 676)—here, "in the chilly darkness," like the NASA astronaut himself. *Driven*

motherships: spaceships that carry and service smaller craft in their cargo. *Matrix of Symbols*

The Mountain of the Adepts: the abode of the gods at the edge of the world. Thus, in the speaker's search for psychological wholeness, "The temple of the wise" is also the "House of the Gathering" or of "Self-Collection" that is "lit by the sun and moon" and that "stands on the seven stages [of alchemical transformation], surmounted by the phoenix [here, both a mythical bird and an emblem of regeneration, resurrection, and immortality]." Significantly, "The temple is hidden in the mountain—a hint that the philosophers' stone [a symbol of the unified self] lies buried in the earth and must be extracted and cleansed." See Jung, *Psychology and Alchemy* 195, fig. 93, and the equally pertinent note on *Self-recollected* given below. *Self-Recollection*

Mount Horeb: a cloud-covered site—usually identified with Mount Sinai—where Moses received the law from God. See Exod. 24.12: "The Lord said to Moses, 'Come up to me on the mountain, stay there and let me give you the tablets of stone, the law and the commandment, which I have written down that you may teach them.'" *Ripples*

multiverse: a concept that derives from a cosmological theory advanced in 1957 by Hugh Everett, and later by Bryce DeWitt, both of whom argue that an infinite number of possible universes (including myriad copies of our local world) comprises but one part of physical reality (Kaku, *Hyperspace* 262-64). *The Quilted Multiverse*

The multiverse *by way of life and mind* / Reflects upon itself: In *Vital Dust: Life as a Cosmic Imperative* (New York: Basic–Harper, 1995), Christian de Duve suggests that "Conscious thought belongs to the cosmological picture, not as some freak epiphenomenon peculiar to our own biosphere, but as a fundamental manifestation of matter" (297). In fact, the very meaning of the universe is to be found in its structure, which produces thought "by way of life and mind" (301). *The Quilted Multiverse*

Murphy's Law: a self-consistent proposition verging on caricature that states that if it is possible for something to go wrong, it will go wrong. *Murphy's Law on Mars*

My implicate eye: a roundabout reference to a new worldview proposed by David Bohm (1917-1994), a renowned theoretical physicist. In this model of reality—as in a hologram—any element contains, enfolded within itself, the totality of the universe. The adjective *implicate,* a neologism, derives from the Latin term *implicare,* to unite, involve, or entangle. Thus, the speaker is, like the postlapsarian Adam, both an "animate being"—an implicated "man made of dust"—and a prospective mirror image of the second Adam, a spiritual man "clothed with immortality." See 1 Cor. 15: 45-49. *Quest*

Mylar: "a polyester made in extremely thin sheets of great tensile strength" ("Mylar" [n.], def.) and used for insulating the NASA spacesuit. The seven layers of Mylar insulation "make the suit act like a thermos" ("Learn about Spacesuits," NASA 13 Nov. 2008: 9 <www.nasa.gov>). *Saturn's Pebble*

myrtle: a plant associated with Aphrodite, the Greek goddess of love and beauty. It has "evergreen leaves, white or pinkish flowers, and dark, fragrant berries" ("Myrtle[1]" [n.], def. 1). *Posthuman*

Mystagogues: persons who interpret religious mysteries or initiate others into them ("Mystagogue" [n.], def.). *Ripples; The Teleoperator's Cue*

My unit manned: the Manned Maneuvering Unit (MMU), a jet backpack that enables an astronaut to fly independently of the shuttle orbiter. See also the note on *Maneuver my unit* given above. *Self-Recollection; The Twin Paradox*

NASA's CAPSTONE: See Kenneth Chang, "NASA's Return to the Moon Starts With Launching a 55-Pound CubeSat," *The New York Times* 27 June 2022: 1 <www.nytimes.com>: "As soon as this week, a spacecraft named CAPSTONE is to launch as the first piece of Artemis [NASA's 21st-century moon program] to head to the moon. Compared to what is to follow, it is modest in size and scope. There won't be any astronauts aboard CAPSTONE. The spacecraft is too tiny, about as big as a microwave oven. This robotic probe won't even land on the moon. [. . .] The full name of the mission is the Cislunar Autonomous Positioning System Technology Operations and Navigation Experiment. It will act as a scout for the lunar orbit where a crewed space station will eventually be built as part of Artemis. That outpost, named Gateway, will serve as a way station where future crews will stop before continuing on to the lunar surface." Chang adds that "CAPSTONE is unusual for NASA in several ways. For one, it is sitting on a launchpad not in Florida but in New Zealand. Second, NASA did not design or build CAPSTONE, nor will it operate it. The agency does not even own it. CAPSTONE belongs to Advanced Space, a 45-employee company on the outskirts of Denver." A final note: CAPSTONE began its near-rectilinear halo orbit (NRHO) of the moon on 13 Nov. 2022. *Eternity's String*

navelstone: the omphalos, the mid-point or navel of the earth—i.e., Golgotha: according to an ancient Christian tradition, both the hill where Adam was buried and the very spot where Christ was crucified. See Jung, *Mysterium Coniunctionis* 388-89. *Link*

Near to the fire: Cf. Jung, *Psychology and Alchemy* 120: "An uncanonical saying of our Lord"—the esoteric Christ—"runs: He who is near unto me is near unto the fire." The quotation is from Aristotle in the *Rosarium philosophorum* (*The Rosary of the Philosophers*), a 16th-century alchemical text. *A Map of the Runner's Route*

Neptune spied on: See Moore, *Travellers in Space and Time* 67: *Neptune* "is too faint to be seen with the naked eye from Earth, but telescopes show a distinct disk, blue instead of green like Uranus." *Habitat*

neurons: "the fundamental units of the brain and nervous system, the cells responsible for receiving sensory input from the external world, for sending motor commands to our muscles, and for transforming and relaying the electrical signals at every step in between. More than that, their interactions define who we are as people." See "What is a neuron?" *Queensland Brain Institute* <https: qbi.uq.edu.au/brain>. *Magellan*

New Heaven's hierophant: "the spiritual, inner and complete man"—the "long-sought" or "sought-after" believer-priest of Isa. 62.12—here taken either as Christ or as the bride of Christ, "the Ransomed of the Lord." See also C. G. Jung, *Mandala Symbolism*, trans. R. F. C. Hull (1959; Princeton: Princeton UP, 1973) 9-10. *Wanderer*

New Heaven's sigil: either "a seal" or "an image or [a] sign supposedly having some mysterious power in magic or astrology" ("Sigil" [n.] defs. 1, 2)—here, alchemy's *spagyric foetus,* both an impasse and a conundrum defined in the explanatory note given below. *Erasure*

Nickel-plated nomad: NASA's Robonaut 2 (R2) is "made from aluminium and nickel-plated carbon fibre," with "four-visible light cameras in its golden head sitting in place of eyes" (Alok Jha, "Meet Robonaut 2, astronaut assistant," *The Guardian* 2 Nov. 2010: 2 <www.theguardian.com/science/2010/nov/02-international-space-station>). *The Teleoperator's Cue*

The nimbus in the lea: in "a meadow or grassy field" ("Lea" [n.], "any rain-producing cloud" ("Nimbus" [n.], def. 1). Here, matched with the restorative powers of the starfish and the mandrake, the transcendent halo of the *nimbus* is also relevant, as in the cloud of light that encircles the head of a god or a saint. *Pioneer*

niobium: "a gray or white metallic chemical element, somewhat ductile and malleable, used in [. . .] jet engines and rockets" ("Niobium" [n.], def.). *Colossus*

Nostoc: in alchemy, "a gelatinous alga that appears after continuous rain. These algae are still known as Nostocs in modern botany. It was earlier supposed that Nostocs fell from the air, or from the stars," like rays that light evinces. Thus, in the "Paracelsan process" of transformation, *Nostoc* "is a sublimating Arcanum, because it comes from heaven" (Jung, *Alchemical Studies* 153n94). *Colossus; Ripples*

noumenon: the essence of an object; in Kantian terms, "the thing in itself," independent of the mind, yet postulated by it. *The Orphan in His Pram*

Nous: in alchemy, not only "the dyestuff or tincture" that "ennobles base substances," but also the pneuma [the life-giving Spirit] that purifies the krater, "the divine vessel" of transformation (Jung, *Psychology and Alchemy* 299). *The Cradle of Life; Exoplanets*

numen: in Roman mythology, "an indwelling guiding force or spirit" ("Numen" [n.], def.). See also *Alchemical Studies* 268, where Jung describes "this moment as a breath of the divine numen." *Lifeworld*

numinous: "having a deeply spiritual or mystical effect" ("Numinous" [adj.], def. 2). *Restoring Hubble's Vision*

obelisk: a shaft of stone—a four-sided pillar—with a tapering pyramidal top; hence, here, both a monolith and a symbol of the human frame. *Habitat; The Skin of the Rocket*

obfuscate: "to cloud over; obscure; make dark or unclear" ("Obfuscate" [vt.], def. 1). *Finger's Grain*

omnibus: here, a molecular self-assembly—a spontaneous compound of atoms. *The Inner Lives of Robots*

omniverse: in current physical cosmology, an infinity of universes—the conglomeration of all possible worlds. *The Embodied Robot; Erasure; Moonplant; The Orphan in His Pram; Rebis; The Shape of Things to Come; Umbilicus*

The omniverse itself implicated: The speaker refers to the implicate order, a new worldview proposed by David Bohm (1917-1994), a renowned theoretical physicist. In this model of reality—as in a hologram—any element contains, enfolded within itself, the totality of the universe. The adjective *implicate,* a neologism, derives from the Latin term *implicare,* to unite, involve or entangle. *The Orphan in His Pram*

Omphale's handmaid, Heaven's feigner: In Greek mythology, Omphale is "a queen of Lydia in whose service Hercules, dressed as a woman, does womanly tasks for three years to appease the gods" ("Omphale" [n.], def.). Hercules had slain "a good friend in order to avenge an insult offered him by the young man's father, King Eurytus" (Hamilton, *Mythology* 168). *Quest; Skein Winder*

omphalos: the mid-point or navel of the earth—Golgotha, according to an ancient Christian tradition, both the hill where Adam was buried and the very spot where Christ was crucified. See Jung, *Mysterium Coniunctionis* 388-89. *The Embodied Robot; Erasure*

Or Athena sprung from the head of Zeus: In Greek myth, *Athena* was "the daughter of Zeus alone" since "No mother bore her." A battle-goddess "full-grown and in full armor," Athena "sprang from his head" (Hamilton, *Mythology* 29). *The Cradle of Life*

orbweb: the gossamer network of the Milky Way compared to a spider's (here, an orb-weaver's) hub of silk. *Moonwalker*

Or disks down inclines merge: an ingenious thought experiment from the Department of Physics and Astronomy at Purdue University—"A collection of disks and hoops, of different radii and different masses, are allowed to roll from rest without slipping down an inclined plane. It is shown that the one that reaches the bottom first depends not on [its] mass or radius, but on [its] shape." See "Demos: 1Q-04 Translation with Rolling" 1 <www.physics.purdue.edu/demos/display>. Last updated 30 Nov. 2023. *Gravity and the Robonaut*

The Orphan in His Pram: here, both an embedded cyborg and a child without parents. The symbolic *Pram* is a baby carriage. *The Orphan in His Pram*

Orthofabric: a material made of three different synthetic fibers (Gore-Tex, Nomex, and Kevlar) and used in constructing the NASA Shuttle spacesuit. *The Shape of Things to Come*

***Ouroboros* (oar-oh-*boar*-ahs):** the snake that bites its own tail—in alchemy, not only a self-described circle, the *opus* that "proceeds from the one and leads back to the one" (Jung, *Psychology and Alchemy* 293 and fig. 147), but also a symbol of totality. *Driven; Link; Magellan; Quest; Scion; Self-Recollection*

Ouroboros' bine: The speaker refers to the twining, winding course of "the self-devouring dragon that [. . .] begot and gave birth to itself," a symbol of alchemical transformation (Jung, *Alchemical Studies* 259). A *bine* is a plant having such a climbing stem. *Link; The Location of Earth; Quest*

Out of His belly: In *Aion* 204-05, Jung reminds us that, like Adam before the creation of Eve, "Christ was supposed by various traditions to be male/female." Thus, medieval iconography "sometimes shows Christ with breasts," in accordance with the Song of Solomon 1.1: "'For thy breasts are better than wine.'" *Eternity's String*

Outrider: "a trailblazer; [a] forerunner" ("Outrider" [n.], def. 3). *The Location of Earth*

pad: here, a launch pad—"the platform from which a rocket, guided missile, etc. is launched" ("Launch Pad," def.). *Copy*

panspermia in space: "a theory holding that seeds of life diffuse naturally through outer space" ("Panspermia" [n.], def.)—in this poem, transported by comets. Of course, on this subject, now, the most accepted theory is biochemical, not cometary, evolution. *Centauri Dreams; The Cradle of Life*

the Paraclete: in the New Testament, "the Holy Spirit, considered as comforter, intercessor, or advocate" ("Paraclete" [n.], def.). See John 14.16, 14.26, 15.26, 16.7, and 1 John 2.1. *A Map of the Runner's Route*

Particle in the Mass: a double allusion—in General Physics, an elementary particle: a piece of matter having negligible size, and in the Roman Catholic Church, a small piece of the Eucharistic host broken off at Mass. See *Saint Joseph Daily Missal* (New York: Catholic Book Publishing Co., 1959) 686-87: In the Holy Sacrifice of the Mass, "The priest breaks the Sacred Host in two. He places one half on the paten [a small plate of precious metal that holds the

Sacred Host, a symbol of Christ's body] and breaks off a particle from the other [. . .]. He puts the particle into the chalice [of wine and water], saying, May this mingling and consecration of the Body and Blood of our Lord Jesus Christ help us who receive it to life everlasting. Amen." (The note on *His body wracked,* given above, is also relevant.) *A Map of the Runner's Route*

Particles fluctuate—slit screen or scrawl: a respectful nod to wave-particle duality and quantum uncertainty. In *Other Worlds: A Portrait of Nature in Rebellion / Space, Superspace and the Quantum Universe* (New York: Simon, 1980), Paul Davies explains that electrons, if liberated, "will spill out in many directions, spreading about like the ripples on a pond" (63). However, in the two-slit experiment, "The interference that occurs [. . .] cannot be between many different electrons, or the pattern would disappear when only one electron is used. It is an interference of probability," i.e., of probability waves (67). In other words, for each electron, both slits "must be left open; either [slit] offers a potential path, though only one can be the actual path. Which one we can never know" (69). Thus, as Jack Sarfatti and Fred Wolf emphasize in *Space-Time and Beyond,* according to the mind-bending concepts of quantum physics, reality may be no more than a function of our "participation with an indefinite number of probabilistic paths" (95). *Sphere*

pasteboard: a Bristol-board—in England, "a stiff material made of layers of paper pasted together" ("Pasteboard" [n.], def. 1) and used by artists and printers. *Scion*

Pathfinder at noon: NASA's second-generation Space Shuttle. Designed "as a technology demonstration of a new way to deliver [both] an instrumented lander and the first-ever robotic rover" to the surface of Mars," *Pathfinder* entered the Martian atmosphere "assisted by a parachute to slow its descent through the thin atmosphere and a giant system of airbags to cushion the impact." It "not only accomplished this goal but also returned an unprecedented amount of data." In fact, from its landing on Mars' Ares Valles on 4 July 1997, until its final data transmission on 27 September 1997, Mars Pathfinder "returned 2.3 billion bits of information, including more than 16,500 images from the lander and 550 images from the rover, as well as more than 15 chemical analyses of rocks and soil and extensive data on winds and other weather factors." See Debra Hernandez, Melody Ho, and Jane Platt, *Mars Pathfinder* 1-3 <https://nasa.gov/mars-exploration/ missions/pathfinder>. Accessed 07 Jan. 2024. *Eternity's String*

peacock: "an early Christian symbol for the Redeemer" (Jung, *Psychology and Alchemy* 419), since its "combination of all colors" signifies wholeness (223). *The Orphan in His Pram; Saturn's Pebble*

Pearls of speech formed within the shells of words: According to Jean Chevalier and Alain Gheerbrant, the pearl is a lunar symbol "linked to water and woman" (*The Penguin Dictionary of Symbols* 742). In addition, the pearl is, "like Plato's spherical man, the image of the ideal perfection of human beings and ends"—in effect, both "the transcendent made amenable to sense-perception" and "the manifestation of God in the Cosmos" (743). In Matthew 13.45-46, the pearl even "stands for the Kingdom of Heaven." Everywhere, in literature, legend, and folklore, "pearls of speech" are symbols "concealed within the shell[s] of words" (744). *Pioneer*

***pelican*:** either the large, web-footed bird with a long, straight bill (a symbol of the salvific Christ) or—because of its resemblance to the *pelican*—an alchemical retort, the philosophical vessel also called, along with the goose [an avatar of the swan] and the stork, "the bird of Hermes [Trismegistus]" (Jung, *Psychology and Alchemy* 370n79). See also Jung, *Alchemical Studies* 87: "Christ himself is the pelican who plucks out his breast feathers for his young." *The Cradle of Life; Lifeworld*

peloton: A *peloton* is "A group of riders that clump together in a bicycle race on the open road"; hence, here—in the root sense of the French word *pelote* from which it derives—a ball or pack or platoon of stars. *Habitat*

perilune: the point nearest to the center of the moon in the orbit of a spacecraft. *Rebis*

phial: "a small glass bottle; [a] vial" ("Phial" [n.], def.). *Posthuman*

Phobos: a Martian moon. Evidently, "Phobos is close enough to Mars that it can collect debris kicked up by major impacts on the Red Planet. [. . .] These samples are likely embedded in the top meter or so of Phobos' surface—a difficult location for robots to sample, but easier for humans." See "Frequently Asked Questions about Humans Orbiting Mars," *The Planetary Society* 14 <hom.planetary.org>. Accessed on 13 May 2017. *Curiosity; The Skin of the Rocket*

phoenix: See Chevalier and Gheerbrant, *The Penguin Dictionary of Symbols* 752: "From the accounts given by Herodotus and Plutarch, the phoenix would seem to have been a mythical bird of matchless splendor and extraordinary longevity which came from Ethiopia and, having been cremated upon a funeral pyre, had the power to be reborn from its own ashes. [. . .] This is why, throughout the Middle Ages, the phoenix was made the symbol of Christ's resurrection and sometimes that of his divine nature." *The Skin of the Rocket*

photon: a messenger particle of the electromagnetic force that, being "massless" (Davies, *The Mind of God* 208), conveys "the smallest bundle of light" (Greene, *The Elegant Universe* 419). *The Embodied Robot; The Location of Earth*

***pinwheel*:** the Milky Way, our own spiral galaxy, a collection of stars, dust, and gas. *Sphere*

Pishon: In Genesis 2.11, one of four murmurous rivers that water the Garden of Eden. The other rivers are Gihon, Tigris, and the Euphrates. The word is pronounced *pea*-shahn. *Habitat*

pixel: "the basic unit or picture element that makes up the image displayed on a video screen" ("Pixel" [n.], def.). *The Teleoperator's Cue*

A plaque with a sign that coheirs subserve: The speaker refers to the *plaque* that NASA launched on March 3, 1972, with the *Pioneer 10* spacecraft. The message, which "is etched on a 6-inch by 9-inch gold-anodized aluminum plate, attached to the antenna support struts of *Pioneer 10*," is meant "to communicate the locale, epoch, and something of the nature of the builders of the spacecraft." Thus, the man depicted raises his right hand as "a 'universal' sign of good will," while the reflective woman, standing, looks on (Carl Sagan and Jerome Agel, *The Cosmic Connection: An Extraterrestrial Perspective* [NewYork: Anchor-Doubleday, 1973] 17-18). Sagan remarks that "The human beings are the most mysterious part of the message" (22). *Pioneer*

pod: a seed case or capsule, as in Mark 4.2-9, where Jesus draws a crowd by a lake-side with a relevant parable: "As he taught he said: 'Listen! A sower went out to sow. And it happened that as he sowed, some seed fell along the footpath; and the birds came and ate it up. Some seed fell on rocky ground, where it had little soil, and it sprouted quickly because it had no depth of earth; but when the sun rose the young corn was scorched, and as it had no root it withered away. Some seed fell among thistles; and the thistles shot up and choked the corn, and it yielded no crop. And then some seed fell into good soil, where it came up and grew, and bore fruit; and the yield was thirtyfold, sixtyfold, even a hundredfold.' He added, 'If you have ears, then hear.'" *Moonplant*

point: According to Johann Christoph Steeb, a Renaissance alchemist, "The point is most akin to the nature of light, and light is a *simulacrum Dei*" (Jung, *Alchemical Studies* 151)—i.e., a trace or a semblance or an image of God. See also *Mysterium Coniunctionis* 45, where Jung quotes another alchemist, John Dee, Steeb's contemporary: "'Things and beings have their first origin in the point and the monad.'" *Sphere*

the poles rotate: i.e., the poles of rotation in plate tectonics. *Wanderer*

Pollux: in Greek and Roman myth, the immortal twin of the mortal Castor. According to Jung, the twins represent the dilemma of the hyphenated God-man. See Jung, *Aion* 81. *The Twin Paradox*

polymer melt: both the viscous liquid state of a *polymer* material that occurs when it is heated above its heating point and a component of the Space Shuttle astronaut's hard upper body case. *Moonplant*

Possess the Savior: Cf. Murray, *The Spirit of Christ:* "There is no way of knowing the Holy Spirit except by possessing Him or being possessed of Him. To live in the Spirit is the only way to know the Spirit" (100). See also *Collect His Scriptures,* an alternate reading of this line given above. *A Map of the Runner's Route*

Posthuman: "Of or relating to a hypothetical species that might evolve from human beings, as by means of genetic or bionic augmentation" (<oed.com/search/dictionary>). See also Francis Fukuyama's caveat in *Our Posthuman Future* (New York: Farrar, Straus, 2002) 14: "Political institutions cannot abolish either nature or nurture altogether and succeed. The history of the twentieth century was defined by two opposite horrors, the Nazi regime, which said biology was everything, and communism, which maintained that it counted for nothing. Liberal democracy has emerged as the only viable and legitimate political system for modern societies because it avoids either extreme, shaping politics to historically created norms of justice while not interfering excessively with natural patterns of behavior," an enlightened moral position that, in this poem, "Heaven's swain" adopts like an "Embedded covenant" (l. 21). *Posthuman*

Preordained Ge's herald, like Noah's dove, / Bears His olive leaf below and above: See Gen. 9.12-17, where God, addressing Noah, sets His bow in the cloud—"sign of the covenant between myself and earth"—even as the faith-based speaker in this poem, parsing the New Covenant and being indwelt, sealed, and Spirit-comforted, walks with the Lord. Chapter 1 in Andrew Murray's *The Spirit of Christ* is also relevant here, along with the note on *Covenant* given above. *The Teleoperator's Cue*

proximal: here, an anatomical term: "situated nearest the center of the body or nearest the point of attachment of a muscle, limb, etc." ("Proximal" [adj.], def. 2). *Scion*

quantum: in the *quantum* theory of matter, a pulse or packet that contains "a given [fixed] quantity of energy" (Paul Davies, *Other Worlds* [New York: Simon, 1980] 32) and that functions as both "wave of probability" (64) and particle. See the note on *Matter is not static: quantum its home* given above. *Umbilicus*

quaternal: a portmanteau word that blends the adjectives "quaternary" (four) and "eternal" (everlasting) and that, in this poem, identifies the otherworldly NASA astronaut as a symbol of the supraordinate "self" (Jung, *The Archetypes and the Collective Unconscious* 187). See the note on *Quaternity's stem* given below. *Quest; The Twin Paradox; Umbilicus*

Quaternity's startlement: See *Aion* 224n7, where Jung remarks that "The circle has the character of wholeness because of its 'perfect' form; the quaternity, because four is the mininum number of parts into which the circle may be naturally divided." Thus, "the quaternity of Christ [. . .] is exemplified by the cross symbol" (204). Here, of course, the speaker responds to an unexpected embodiment of the God-image: "Adam before the Fall" (39). *Rebis*

Quaternity's stem: the upright human body, an image of the total self. See *Aion* 224n7, where Jung remarks that "The circle has the character of wholeness because of its 'perfect' form; the quaternity, because four is the minimum number of parts into which the circle may be naturally divided." Thus, "the quaternity of Christ [. . .] is exemplified by the cross symbol" (204), the latter icon, in Jungian texts, a symbol of *discriminated* wholeness, since it subsumes the four psychological functions: sensation and intuition; thinking and feeling. *Eternity's String; Skein Winder; Umbilicus*

quicksilver: in alchemy, a metal that is not only fluid like water (Jung, *Alchemical Studies* 207) and concrete like silver (Jung, *The Archetypes and the Collective Unconscious* 312), but also "penetrating like spirit-substance" (*Alchemical Studies* 297). *Magellan; The Skin of the Rocket*

quill: a pen for writing made from "the hollow, horny stem of a feather" ("Quill" [n.], defs. 2, 4). *The Mill of the Host*

The Quilted Multiverse: an infinite universe composed, like a gigantic quilt, of patchwork parallel universes (Brian Greene, *The Hidden Reality: Parallel Universes and the Deep Laws of the Cosmos* [New York: Vintage-Random, 2011] 355). *The Quilted Multiverse*

***quinces*:** "golden or greenish-yellow, hard, apple-shaped fruit of a small tree (*Cydonia oblonga*) of the rose family" ("Quince" [n.], def. 1). *Gravity and the Robonaut*

qwiff: a quantum wave function that describes "the probability of an observation and not the actual observation" (Fred Alan Wolf, *Taking the Quantum Leap* [New York: Harper, 1981] 170). However, according to Wolf, it is the human perceiver who activates the *qwiff*—i.e., turns it on and off—and, with each observation, collapses the wave of probability into reality. *Lifeworld; The Twin Paradox*

A radar mapper bound for Venus' run: NASA's Magellan Mission to planet Venus was completed on 15 May 1991, after 243 days of continuous mapping with the Synthetic Radar (SAR), altimeter, and passive radiometer, "all based on the same radar system and multiplexing three types of measurements." The mission resulted in "an unprecedented volume of 1,650 image strips covering 84 percent of the planet's surface," a data set that is "unique for any planet." See "Radargrammetric Measurements from the Initial Magellan Coverage of Planet Venus," *Photogrammetric Engineering and Remote Sensing,* vol. 57, December 1991: 1561-1570. *Magellan*

the raker: the Grim Reaper—"death, often personified as a shrouded skeleton bearing a scythe" ("Reaper" [n.], def. 2). *The Cutting Edge of Haptics*

rebis (*ray*-bis or *ray*-beese): a basic alchemical symbol. "[C]ompounded of two parts and therefore frequently hermaphroditic as an amalgam of Sol and Luna," the *rebis* depicts "the consciousness-transcending fact [that] we call the self" (Jung, *Psychology and Alchemy* 202). *Centauri Dreams; Copy; The Cradle of Life; Driven; Erasure; The Location of Earth; The Mill of the Host; The Moon in Transition Raised to the Sun; Moonplant; Moonwalker; Murphy's Law on Mars; The Orphan in His Pram; Quest; The Quilted Multiverse; Rebis; The Skin of the Rocket; The Twin Paradox; Wanderer.*

Redemption is a work: See the note on *the Host in the Mill* given above. *The Mill of the Host*

redshifted in my race: See Kaku, *Hyperspace* 196: "the fact that the stars are receding from us at fantastic velocities has been repeatedly verified by measuring the distortion of their starlight (called the red shift)." The author adds that "The starlight of a receding star is shifted to longer wavelengths—that is, toward the red end of the spectrum—in the same way that the whistle of a receding train sounds higher than normal when approaching and lower when receding. This is called the Doppler effect," a phenomenon named after C. J. Doppler (1803-53), an Austrian Physicist. *The Twin Paradox*

reify His mime: Like an actor skilled in pantomime, the spiritually fragile speaker imitates the life of Christ. *A Map of the Runner's Route*

reinforced his boots: For exploration on Mars, the boots will have to contain "a material with a high level of radiation resistance." Furthermore, "The sole of the boots will need to be quite stiff [in order] to accommodate any uneven ground that the astronauts will need to traverse." Since "much of the Martian surface is mountainous," crampons could be required

(Stuart Morgan, "Footwear in Space," *SATRA Bulletin* 18 Nov. 2019: 6 <www.satra.com/bulletin/article.php=2387)>. *Pioneer*

remnant in the froth: the tabernacled NASA astronaut perceived as one of End-time's "ransomed" believer-priests, whom the Lamb, having come again to judge the living and the dead, shall "glide or pass swiftly and lightly over" (Rev. 14.3-5). *Driven*

Remnant of a sign that athanors grind: See Jung, *Alchemical Studies* B4: "The figure in the middle is Eve (earth), who is reunited with Adam (Christ) in the coniunctio. From their union is born the hermaphrodite, the incarnate Primordial Man. To the right is the athanor (furnace) with the vessel in the centre, from which the lapis (hermaphrodite) will arise. The vessels on either side contain Sol and Luna." *Restoring Hubble's Vision*

repairs cracked stringers: i.e., the damaged support beams in the space shuttle Discovery's external fuel tank. See Steven Siceloff, "Technicians Use Scanners to Survey External Tank," along with the accompanying image: "Technicians use spray foam insulation on space shuttle Discovery's external tank to cover [. . .] repaired stringers," *NASA – Space Shuttle* 23 Nov. 2010: 1-2 <nasa.com>. *The Moon in Transition Raised to the Sun*

Residual coupling: In *Other Worlds*, Davies remarks that, in Newton's clockwork universe, reality "is perceived as a collection of distinct objects in interaction with one another. The idea is, however, only approximate. Objects are distinct so long as their mutual interaction is in some vague sense small. When a drop of liquid falls into the ocean it interacts strongly with the larger body of water and becomes absorbed into it, losing its identity completely. To take another example, a foetus only gradually acquires a separate identity from the mother as it grows in the womb. Generally speaking, when objects are separated by a large distance, we think of them as being distinct: the planets of the solar system, the atoms in London and New York, etc. This is because all known forces of interaction diminish rapidly with distance, so that well-separated entities behave almost independently. They are never, of course, completely independent—there is always a residual coupling between all things—but the concept of distinct, separate objects is a very useful one in practice" (109). *A Map of the Runner's Route*

Resin: here, not only a component of the Space Shuttle astronaut's hard upper body case, but also the resin of the wise, "a synonym for the transforming substance," either the life force likened by the alchemists "to the glue of the world" or a red gum [originally gum Arabic] fixed as "the medium between mind and body and the union of both" (Jung, *Psychology and Alchemy* 161). See also Chevalier and Gheerbrant, *The Penguin Dictionary of Symbols* 797: "Because it is incorruptible, because it is flammable, and because it is generally produced by evergreen trees [including such conifers as the spruce, the fir, the cedar, and the pine], resin is a symbol of purity and immortality." In fact, "The trees from which it comes have sometimes been taken as symbols of Christ." *Moonplant*

resonant strings: See Brian Greene, *The Elegant Universe: Superstrings, Hidden Dimensions, and the Quest for the Ultimate Theory* 143-44: "According to string theory, the properties of an elementary 'particle'—its mass and its various force charges—are determined by the precise resonant pattern of vibration that its internal string [i.e., its incredibly tiny, one-dimensional filament] executes." *Self-Recollection*

Right-handed, left-handed my foetus curled: In the Cabalistic view, "Man and his heavenly prototype are twins" (Jung, *Mysterium Coniunctionis* 413n198). *Umbilicus*

ring: Here, the titular "runner" alludes not only to the Anthropos, in alchemy the "round, original form" of "the spiritual, inner and complete man" (Jung, *Mandala Symbolism* 9-10), but also to the birth of the self (24). *A Map of the Runner's Route*

ringers: the plural form of *ringer*: either "any substitute" or "a person or thing very closely resembling another" ("Ringer"[2] [n.], defs. 1b and 1c) or, simply enough, a robot clone. *The Moon in Transition Raised to the Sun*

ripples: gravitational waves that formed in the violent expansion of the universe after the Big Bang. *Ripples*

riven God: Christ, sundered by violent yet voluntary death from the Father. See Heb. 7.27: Jesus "has no need to offer sacrifices daily, as the high priests do, first for his own sins and then for those of the people; for this he did once and for all when he offered up himself." *Link*

Robonaut: NASA's robotic astronaut, a "state-of-the-art humanoid" designed for space travel. "Outside the spacecraft, it will perform its tasks under the control of a human operator at a tele-presence console" (Peter Menzel and Faith D'Aluisio, *Robo sapiens: Evolution of a New Species* [Cambridge: MIT P, 2000] 129). See also Julia Badger and Ron Diftler, "Robonaut 2," *Robonaut-NASA,* 20 Sept. 2019 (<robonaut.jsc.nasa.gov>), a useful update on the subject. Thus, having been "upgraded by the addition of two climbing manipulators ('legs'), *Robonaut* 2 (R2) is now capable of speeds more than four times faster than *Robonaut* 1 (R1), "is more compact [and] more dexterous," and includes such advanced features as series elastic joint technology, extended finger and thumb travel, miniaturized load cells, redundant force sensing, [and also] ultra high-speed joint controllers" (1-2). In earlier configurations, *Robonaut* had used "a single 'space leg' to move around the outside of a simulated Space Station" and then, later, even "glided from one test station to another" on a Segway scooter "with gyro-stabilized wheels" Fraser Cain, "NASA's Robonaut Can Move Around Now," *Universe Today,* 9 August 2004 (<www.universetoday.com/9803>). See also the note on *Segway* given below. *Finger's Grain; Gravity and the Robonaut; In the Outposts of Space; The Teleoperator's Cue*

Robonaut's crow: a disturbing image, since Robonaut 2 is linked to the raven as either "a symbol of clear-sightedness" or "a messenger of of death" (Chevalier and Gheerbrant, *The Penguin Dictionary of Symbols* 789). *Finger's Grain*

rockface that freights: here, a vertical surface of rock, as on a mountainside, that carries "the sculpture of a human face cut into the rock about 2,000 years ago. See Abraham Sankaran, "Mysterious ancient 'human face' rock carvings revealed by receding waters in [the Brazilian] Amazon," *Independent* 25 Oct. 2023: 4 <independent.co.uk/news/science/archeology>). *The Cradle of Life*

rod: "a staff, scepter, etc., carried as a symbol of office, rank, or power" ("Rod" [n.], def. 5a). *Link; Moonplant*

Rose-colored eros: Jung identifies the source of this allusion in *Alchemical Studies* 295: "It seems as though the rose-colored blood of the alchemical redeemer was derived from a rose mysticism that penetrated into alchemy, and that, in the form of the red tincture, it expressed the healing or whole-making effect of a certain kind of Eros." See also the note on *rosy sweat* given below. *The Skin of the Rocket*

rosy sweat: i.e., in alchemy, the bloody *sweat* of the philosophic stone, a parallel of Christ in the garden of Gethsemane. Jung notes that "This man will appear on earth only 'in the last days.' He cannot be Christ, for Christ by his blood has already redeemed the world from the consequences of the Fall. [. . .] On no account is it a question here of a future Christ and *salvator microcosmi,* but rather of the alchemical *servator cosmi* (preserver of the cosmos), representing the still unconscious idea of the whole and complete man, who shall bring about what the sacrificial death of Christ has obviously left unfinished, namely the deliverance of the world from evil. Like Christ, he will sweat a redeeming blood, but [. . .] it is 'rose-colored'; not natural or ordinary blood but symbolic blood, the manifestation of a certain kind of Eros which unifies the individual as well as the multitude in the sign of the rose and makes them whole" (*Alchemical Studies* 295-96). *Colossus*

rotundum: in alchemy, the "round, original form" of "the spiritual, inner, and complete man" (Jung, *Mandala Symbolism* 9-10). *Rebis*

Round as the Self, yet quaternal His sod: See the note on *Quaternity's stem* given above. *Eternity's String*

rover: See the note on *sky crane* given below. *The Teleoperator's Cue*

rune: "any poem, verse, or song, esp[ecially] one that is mystical or obscure" ("Rune" [n.], def. 3b). Evidently, the speaker views spaceflight as a spiritual quest. *Eternity's String; Link; Moonwalker*

sacerdotal: "priestly" ("Sacerdotal" [adj.], def. 1). *The Teleoperator's Cue*

Sagittarius: the constellation that "lies in the direction of the center of the Milky Way and is filled with star clouds and patches of light which are resolved by a telescope into clusters and nebulae" (Engelbrektson, *Stars, Planets, and Galaxies* 35). *Skein Winder*

salt: See Jung, *The Archetypes and the Collective Unconscious* 328, where "Salt, in ecclesiastical as well as alchemical usage, is the symbol [. . .] for the distinguished or elect personality," i.e., an analogue of the God-man, as in Matthew 5.13: "'You are salt to the world.'" *Erasure; Rebis; The Twin Paradox*

Saturn fed / On Gaea's biped: The Roman god *Saturn* was one of the Titans, the same as the Greek god Cronus. In this poem, *Gaea's biped*—an imagined *future* version of NASA's Robonaut 2—is a stand-in for Rhea's son, Zeus. In fact, the speaker evokes a well-known, cosmogonic Greek myth. Thus, when "Cronus, the lord of the universe, had learned that one of his children was destined some day to dethrone him, he rebelled against his fate by swallowing them as soon as they were born." However, "when Rhea bore Zeus, her sixth child, she succeeded in having him secretly carried off to Crete, while she gave her husband a great stone wrapped in swaddling clothes which he supposed was the baby and swallowed down accordingly." Nevertheless, later, "when Zeus was grown, he forced his father with the help of his grandmother, the Earth, to disgorge" the anointed stone "along with the five earlier children" (Hamilton, *Mythology* 65-66). Of course, here, even as in a succeeding line the "foetus steers," the mythic fate of rival species evolves anew. *The Moon in Transition Raised to the Sun; Saturn's Pebble; The Shape of Things to Come*

Saturn: rocket in the bind: here, the *Saturn* V rocket that NASA used, during the 1960s and 1970s, to send Apollo astronauts to the moon. *Magellan; Scion; The Teleoperator's Cue*

Saturn's pebble: See the note on *Saturn fed / On Gaea's biped* given above. *Saturn's Pebble*

Saturn's stark pictures with rings that unnerve: The icy rings of the planet Saturn "face the earth every 15 years, alternately showing the northern and the southern hemisphere. When the rings are seen edge-on, they disappear, indicating a thickness of merely a few miles" (Engelbrektson, *Stars, Planets, and Galaxies* 104). *Pioneer*

Saul's magus: "a sorcerer or [an] astrologer" ("Magus" [n.], def. 2)—here, Jesus Christ, the Son of God. In a "Diploma Thesis" completed for the C. G. Jung Institute in 1996, John Granrose observes that "Christ has often been viewed as a kind of magician." Thus, "many older illustrations show Jesus using a magic wand of some kind to perform his miracles. For example, [a] Fourth Century image from the Vatican library shows Jesus raising Lazarus from the dead by touching him with a type of wand" ("The Archetype of the Magician," 2 May 2017: 13 <www.granrose.com>). Incidentally, in early Christian texts, the apostle Paul, being a Roman citizen, was also known as Saul, the Latin equivalent of his name. *Posthuman*

scarab: In Egyptian mythology, the unicorned sun-beetle symbolizes "both the Sun's cycle and, at the same time, resurrection" (Chevalier and Gheerbrant, *The Penguin Dictionary of Symbols* 833). See also *Psychology and Alchemy* 452, where Jung indicates that the *scarab* is "a creature born of itself." *A Map of the Runner's Route*

the scimitar by the scabbard owned: The speaker describes the encased blade of a short, curved sword. *Clotho's Thrum*

scion: "a descendant; [an] offspring" ("Scion," [n.], def. 2)—here, of both Christ and Abraham. See Gal. 3.26: "For through faith you are all sons of God in union with Christ Jesus. Baptized into union with him, you have all put on Christ as a garment. There is no such thing as Jew and Greek, slave and freeman, male and female; for you are all one person in Christ Jesus. But if you thus belong to Christ, you are the 'issue' of Abraham, and so heirs by promise." *Copy; The Embodied Robot; Exoplanets; Finger's Grain; Rebis; Scion*

Scion regimented as a crystal: In his *Homiliae in Ezechielem* (*Homilies on Ezekiel*), Saint Gregory the Great [c. 540-604] explains that, through the "glory" of His resurrection, Christ "'hardened after the fashion of a crystal from water, so that there was one and the same nature in it and in [H]im [. . .]'" (qtd. in Jung, *Mysterium Coniunctionis* 449n345). *Scion*

scoriae: the refuse from the melting of metals. *The Twin Paradox*

scree: a pile of loose stones or rocky detritus lying at the foot of a hill or at the base of a cliff. *Saturn's Pebble*

scrim: "a hanging [of a light, sheer, loosely woven cotton or linen cloth] used in theatrical productions either as an opaque backdrop or as a semitransparent curtain, depending on the lighting" ("Scrim" [n.], defs. 1 and 2). *The Cutting Edge of Haptics; Hyperspace*

Scripted like a wave: i.e., like the quantum Christ described by a specific wavefunction—here, by probability waves: the units of information encoded in an isolated system of multiple particles, whereby observer, observed, and the "presentness" of all experienced moments are part of physical reality. See Davies, *Other Worlds* 63-69, 127, and 190. *The Mill of the Host*

seahorse that floats amid frond or fan: In this passage, the speaker who "sought to be neither woman nor man, / But both these sexes" (lines 4-5) refers, without irony, to the amazing pregnancy of the male *seahorse*. Thus, after the female fish "lays her eggs in an armored chamber (marsupium) of his belly, the sperm-producing male "fertilizes the eggs"; broods them "for about four weeks, while they are nourished by secretions from the spongy wall of his brood pouch"; and then, "over a period of 24 hours, [. . .] undergoes a series of shuddering contractions," even as "the perfectly formed young seahorses are expelled in large numbers" (Jane Reynolds, Phil Gates, and Gaden Robinson, *365 Days of Nature and Discovery* [New York: Abrams, 1994] 108). *Rebis*

the Sea of Showers: i.e., Mare Imbrium, a vast lava plain formed when an asteroid collided with the Moon 3.9 billion years ago. *Link*

the Segway that he prizes: the Robotic Mobility Platform (RMP), both a "two-wheeled vehicle [that] can balance and hold position, while driving front to back and turning," and a lower body on wheels designed for Robonaut 2. See Joe Bibby and Ryan Necessary, "Robonaut 1: RMP [Robotic Mobility Platform]," *NASA* 13 Mar. 2008: 1-2 <robonaut.jsc.nasa.gov>. The note on *Ge's interstellar Centaur*, given above, is also pertinent. *Gravity and the Robonaut*

Selene: a benevolent Greek moon-goddess. Her lover was Endymion, the androgynous shepherd. According to Edith Hamilton, in Greek lore, the Moon is the goddess with three forms: "Selene in the sky [the full moon], Artemis on earth [the day-moon], [and] Hecate in the lower world and in the world above when it is wrapped in darkness" (*Mythology* 31). *The Cutting Edge of Haptics; Moonwalker; Quest; Wanderer*

Selene's cyborg imbued by the light: both the moon-entwined Savior, the "joyful Giant" of line 1, and the faith-based believer-priest of line 24. *Wanderer*

Selene's mound: in Greek myth, the cave on Mount Latmos, where each night Selene, the moon-goddess, visits Endymion, her immortal shepherd-lover. *The Cutting Edge of Haptics*

Self: "the [divine] archetype of unity" (Jung, *Psychology and Alchemy* 25); "the life force that eternally renews itself" and that is like "the [cosmic] clock that never runs down" (120). *Eternity's String*

The Self is a storey, tower or house, / Ziggurat, rubble: "the life force that eternally renews itself" (Jung, *Psychology and Alchemy* 120) compared to the specific level of a building; or to a sacred structure raised to heaven; or to a dwelling place: a private habitation; or to a tiered temple tower with a shrine at the top; or, simply enough, to rough, irregular, loose fragments of rock. See also Christ the "rock of refuge" addressed in Ps. 71.3; the believer who builds his house on rock described in Matt. 7.24-25 and even apotheosized in John 10.34-38, and the note on *Self* given above. *The Mill of the Host*

Self-recollected: In *Psychology and Western Religion* (trans. R. F. C. Hull [Princeton: Princeton UP, 1984]), C. G. Jung examines the crucial (psychological) phenomenon identified here, that of self-recollection. Thus, "the integration or humanization of the self is initiated from the conscious side," he asserts, "by our making ourselves aware of our selfish aims; we examine our motives and try to form as complete and objective a picture as possible of our own nature. It is an act of self-recollection, a gathering together of what is scattered, of all the things in us that have never been properly related, and coming to terms with [ourselves] with a view to achieving full consciousness." Jung maintains that "we are forced to make this effort by the unconscious presence of the self, which is all the time urging us to overcome our unconsciousness" (159). *A Map of the Runner's Route*

Self-Recollection: See the note on *Self-recollected* given above. *Self-Recollection*

Self's trespass—aseity in the act: Aseity is "The divine attribute of uncaused existence" (*Catholic Dictionary* [catholicculture.org>]). Thus, "Creatures exist as effects of other beings and ultimately of God; they are therefore 'from another' (*ab alio*). But God exists of himself (*a se*); he is wholly self-actualized" (Etym. Latin *a*, from + *se*, self). *The Inner Lives of Robots*

a shade / Tabernacled: "a ghost; a specter" ("Shade" [n.], def. 7a). However, here, Jesus is *Tabernacled*, i.e., "sacramentally present in the eucharistic mystery" even as "the merits of the Passion of Christ are applied to our souls" (Thomas Merton, *The Living Bread* [New York: Dell, 1959] 25, 61). *Self-Recollection*

the Shade in the scheme: here, the dusky spirit or soul of the baptized sinner. See Romans 6.5-14, where Paul refers to the moral anarchists who became "slaves of righteousness", i.e., "dead men raised to life" as devout witnesses to the resurrected Christ. *Eternity's String*

Shadow that we shun: the inky darkness that pervades the cosmos, as well as the proclivity to evil that contaminates human nature. Jung illuminates the archetype of the shadow in *Aion*: "The shadow is a moral problem that challenges the whole ego-personality, for no one can become conscious of the shadow without considerable moral effort. To become conscious of it involves recognizing the dark aspects of the personality as present and real. This act is essential for any kind of self-knowledge [. . .]" (8). *The Location of Earth*

Shaman (shah-mun): either a priest or a magus or a holy man with supernatural powers. *Erasure; The Location of Earth; The Orphan in His Pram; Posthuman; The Quilted Multiverse; Self-Recollection; Sphere*

the shaman that wives: According to Jung, in the literature of the alchemists, "the climbing of the magical tree," a universal symbol of both the innermost personality and the transpersonal self, is also "the heavenly journey of the shaman, during which he encounters his heavenly spouse," i.e., his anima (*Alchemical Studies* 303), a "union of opposites" (341) that leads to the integration of the conscious and the unconscious and thereafter to the enlightened goal of the opus: the self-actualized "individuation of the adept" (326). *Posthuman*

shard: "a fragment or broken piece, esp. of pottery" ("Shard" [n.], def. 1). *Scion*

She [. . .] designs his pod: here, a fanciful trope: Gaia, in Greek myth an Earth goddess, has engineered a portable habitat built for Mars—specifically, the Bigelow Expandable Activity Module, or BEAM, "a 3,086-pound pod made of layers of fabric and Kevlar-like material that one day might be able to house astronauts during deep-space missions, and possibly even space tourists on sightseeing trips." See Lonnie Shekhtman, "Why was an inflatable pod just attached to the Space Station?" *The Christian Science Monitor* 18 Apr. 2016: 2 <www.csmonitor.com>. *Link*

a shell in its hand: i.e., a seashell, a Stone Age symbol of rebirth (Chevalier and Gheerbrant, *The Penguin Dictionary of Symbols* 871). *Saturn's Pebble*

Shem: In the "mythologized ethnology" of Genesis, *Shem* is both the eldest son of Noah and the "eponymous" ancestor "of the Hebrews and their various cognates" (Bernard E. Lewis, "Who Are the Semites?" *My Jewish Learning* [n.d.]: 1 <www.myjewishlearning.com>). Thus, in Psalm 45.7, *Shem* is an "anointed" precursor of the Messiah, and, in Luke 3.36, Jesus is a descendant of *Shem*. *Eternity's String*

Sheol (she-ohl): In *Handbook to the Gospels* (Ann Arbor, Michigan: Servant Books), John Wijngaards helpfully discriminates between the hell of the eternally damned and *Sheol*, "'the place of the dead,' the home (in Jewish theology) of all the dead [. . .]. When we say that Jesus descended into hell we mean only (in the terminology of the Bible) that he was truly dead; he was no longer in the 'land of the living' but went down into the 'land of the dead'" (244-45), as every sojourner must. *Link; Self-Recollection*

Shriven: "to get absolution for oneself by confessing" ("Shriven" [vt.], def. 2). *Finger's Grain*

shuttle: here, NASA's space *shuttle*, "a manned, airplanelike spacecraft designed for shuttling back and forth, as between the earth and a space station, transporting personnel and equipment" ("Space Shuttle" [def.]. *The Teleoperator's Cue*

Siloam: in John 9.1-7, the Pool of *Siloam,* where Jesus cured a blind man. *Self-Recollection*

Silver Argiope: The floating NASA astronaut likened to the *Argiope,* the "large, conspicuous" spider that hangs "head down" in the center of its web, which "usually has crossed zigzag bands" (Herbert W. Levi, Lorna R. Levi, and Herbert S. Zim, *A Guide to Spiders and Their Kin* [New York: Golden Press, 1968] 68-69, with haunting illustrations by Nicholas Strekalovsky). *Erasure*

Silver residue: in alchemy, "the white elixir of silver," here likened to Woman as the essence of the "philosophical" gold (Jung, *Alchemical Studies* 135n7), "a purer form of Man." *The Shape of Things to Come*

the Simon that shrives: "Peter, the Rock" (Matt. 16.18), the "favored" apostle. However, in John 20.22-23, all twelve disciples receive the power to "forgive any man's sins." *Posthuman*

Since the Self reflects both matter and Zen: The speaker recalls "a variety of Buddhism, now practiced esp[ecially] in Japan, Vietnam, and Korea," that seeks "to attain an intuitive illumination of mind and spirit, through meditation," in particular "on paradoxes" ("Zen" [n.], def. 1). *The Twin Paradox*

Singularity's dot: in astrophysics, the point of infinite compression at which space and time cease to exist. Here, the serpentine *dot* also evokes the symbol of the crowned Ouroboros, "the snake that bites its own tail," the latter image both a self-described circle and a symbol of totality (Jung, *Aion* 190). *Quest; Saturn's Pebble*

skein: "a quantity of thread or yarn wound in a coil" ("Skein" [n.], def. 1a). See also the note on *Space or skein* given below. *Clotho's Thrum; Finger's Grain; Hyperspace; Link; Moonplant; The Orphan in His Pram; Skein Winder; The Teleoperator's Cue*

skim: floating matter formed on the surface of a liquid. *Eternity's String*

skin of the waker: either the resurrected Christ or His believer-priest, the speaker himself: "in the secret place" the new temple where Christ Himself dwells (Murray, *The Spirit of Christ* 211). *The Cutting Edge of Haptics*

sky crane: NASA's Perseverance rover landed on Mars in February 2021 with the same *sky crane* maneuver that the Curiosity rover used in August 2012: "A sweeping robotic jetpack delivered Curiosity to its landing area and lowered it to the surface with nylon ropes, then cut the ropes and flew off to conduct a controlled crash landing safely out of range of the rover" (2). However, during the landing of Perseverance, "the sky crane was even more precise. The addition of something called *tension relative navigation* enabled the SUV-size rover to touch down safely in an ancient lake bed riddled with rocks and craters" (3). See Andrew Good, Karen Fox, and Alana Johnson, "How Curiosity's Sky Crane Changed the Way NASA Explores Mars", *NASA Jet Propulsion Laboratory,* 7 August 2024 <jpl.nasa.gov/news>. *Matrix of Symbols; The Teleoperator's Cue*

slough of the cobra: an ambivalent image, yet in this stanza, like rock and glass, "the sacred made manifest" (Chevalier and Gheerbrant, *The Penguin Dictionary of Symbols* 845). *Clotho's Thrum*

Smaller than small: The speaker refers to the Child, a numinous symbol, since, as "bringers of light, that is, enlargers of consciousness, child-figures overcome darkness, which is to say that they overcome the earlier unconscious state." Thus, according to Jung, "'Child' means something evolving toward independence," a "nascent state of consciousness. So long as this is not actually in being, the 'child' remains a mythological projection which requires religious repetition and renewal by ritual. The Christ Child, for instance, is a religious necessity only so long as the majority of men are incapable of giving psychological reality to the saying: 'Except ye become as little children. . . .'" Not surprisingly, then, "the 'child' distinguishes itself by deeds which point to the conquest of the dark" (*The Archetypes and the Collective Unconscious* 166-71). *A Map of the Runner's Route*

The snow-flecked soul: the purified spirit, like the mercurial life-force, "flies like solid white snow" (Jung, *Alchemical Studies* 214). *Skein Winder*

The sole artifex of the eternal: the Christian artist predicated as coheir, priest, and scribe. See Jung, *Psychology and Alchemy* 283, fig. 141: "The artifex with book and altar." *Skein Winder*

solstice: "The origin of the word solstice means '(the) sun has stood (still).' The sun reaches the solstices on June 21 and December 21 in the solar calendar employed in many countries throughout the world. Generally, in the northern hemisphere, the June solstice is called the summer solstice and the December solstice [is called] the winter solstice" (Engelbrektson, *Stars, Planets, and Galaxies* 14). *Habitat*

Sol's verve: In this poem, Sol is "the rising sun—the *Sol mysticus*," i.e., the pre-existent Christ: "the reborn as his own begetter" (Jung, *Symbols of Transformation* 322-23). *Pioneer*

Some archaic species: click-speaker clay: the Khoikhoi and Bushmen, the first people of southern Africa. A notable feature of their languages is "the use of clicks as consonants" (William A. Haviland, et al., *Cultural Anthropology: The Human Challenge* [15th ed.; Boston: Cengage Learning, 2017] xxx). *Wanderer*

Some azure planet: a picture of the Earth taken in 1990 at a distance of about 3.7 billion miles by the Voyager 1 space probe—the home *planet* that, at the time, Carl Sagan, a space scientist, famously dubbed a "pale blue dot" and that he later described as "a mote of dust suspended in a sunbeam" in *Pale Blue Dot: A Vision of the Human Future in Space* (New York: Random-Ballantine, 1994) 6. See also Elizabeth Landau, "'Pale Blue Dot' Images Turn 25," *NASA Jet Propulsion Laboratory* 13 Feb. 2015: 1-4 <www.jpl.nasa.gov>. *Clotho's Thrum*

Some solar raven: In Lev. 11.13-15 and in Luke 12.24, the *raven*—like the crow an ambivalent bird—is yet "cognitively calpable." See the note on *Ge's self-abstracted crow* given above. *Self-Recollection*

Sophia's flow: in Gnostic doctrine, Sophia is "the mother or bride of Christ" (Jung, *Psychology and Alchemy* 404). She also corresponds to Luna, the mother of the night (Jung, *Mysterium Coniunctionis* 355), and to the Holy Ghost (454). In fact, elsewhere, "the *filii Sapientiae*, the philosophers, drink" from the breasts of the maternal Sophia (Jung, *Alchemical Studies* 308). *Exoplanets*

So suns and moons conjoin: a syzygy (*siz*-uh-jee), paired opposites that represent wholeness—for example, Male and Female, as in the symbol of the hermaphroditic *rebis*, the God-image "compounded of two parts and therefore," according to the medieval alchemists, "frequently [. . .] an amalgam of Sol and Luna" (Jung, *Psychology and Alchemy* 202). *Gravity and the Robonaut*

So, Typhon pursuing him, Pisces shunts / In the wettest place that the foetus fronts: In Greek mythology, *Typhon,* the monster with a hundred heads, had pursued Leto when her son Apollo "was still in her womb; but she fled to the floating island of Delos on a 'night sea journey' and was there safely delivered of her child" (Jung, *Symbols of Transformation* 371). Here, of course, *Pisces,* who *shunts* or turns aside in order to conquer the serpent, represents not only Christ, both sun-hero and "Goat-Fish," but also His womb-entwining coheir, the speaker himself. In other words, the latterday galactic pilgrim, being reborn, has just emerged—like the Son of God—from "'the wettest place on earth,' [. . .] the maternal depths" (198). *Rebis*

soul-sparks: In esoteric teachings of rabbinical origin, the Son of God "descends into matter" in the form of *soul-sparks* "and then frees himself from [matter] in order to bring healing and salvation to all souls" (Jung, *Psychology and Alchemy* 301). *Curiosity; Exoplanets; Hyperspace; Gravity and the Robonaut; The Shape of Things to Come*

Space or skein: a mathematical set: spacetime conceived as a *mathematical* model that fuses the three dimensions of space and the one dimension of time into a single four-dimensional continuum. In this passage, *skein* refers to our cosmic narrative thread, which may well be but a self-excited *mathematical* construct and not a real thing. *Eternity's String; Skein Winder*

Spacetime damped down before its Spirals char: There are about 70-80 billion spiral galaxies that rotate like pinwheels in the observable universe. The Milky Way is an example of a spiral galaxy that contains our solar system. *Umbilicus*

Spacetime is objective: forged in the stars, / Everywhere is the same—it has no bars: The speaker refers to the cosmological principle, which states that, "when local irregularities are ignored, or averaged out, the universe at any instant in time is the same everywhere in space." See Edward Harrison, *Masks of the Universe* (New York: MacMillan, 1985) 174-75. Not insignificantly, in "God Is Also a Cosmologist," Margaret Wertheim, quoting Professor Harrison, reminds us that, sometimes, science "verges on theology" (*The New York Times* 8 June 1997: 3 <nytimes.com>). *Cosmologist*

Spacetime's horn antenna: In 1965 Arno Penzias and Robert Wilson "made one of the greatest discoveries in 500 years of modern astronomy. By accident, they discovered the cosmic fireball radiation that [Ralph] Alpher and [Robert] Herman had predicted. The discovery was made with [a] large horn antenna [. . .]. The horn, built like an oversized ear trumpet, is sensitive to faint radio whispers that travel through the universe. Penzias and Wilson were not looking for clues to the beginning of the world when they made their discovery. While testing their equipment, they noticed an unexplained static coming out of their radio receiver." Eventually they realized that they had detected "radiation left over from the fireball that filled the Universe at the beginning of its existence" (Jastrow, *God and the Astronomers* 20). *Magellan*

The spagyric foetus: The word *spagyric* refers to an alchemical process that both separates and combines (Jung, *Mysterium Coniunctionis* 481n91). Thus, the *spagyric foetus* ascends into Heaven that it may become a spirit from a body and then descends to earth that it may become a body again. Elsewhere, Jung explains that "The spagyric birth (*spagyrica foetura*) is nothing other than the *filius philosophorum,* the inner, eternal man in the shell of the outer, mortal man" (*Alchemical Studies* 150). Cf. John 3.13: "No one ever went up into heaven except the one who came down from heaven, the Son of Man whose home is in heaven." *The Cradle of Life; Curiosity; Erasure; The Location of Earth; The Orphan in His Pram; Quest; The Quilted Multiverse; Ripples; Saturn's Pebble; The Skin of the Rocket; The Teleoperator's Cue*

spagyric gum: *gum* Arabic, or "blessed" red *gum,* not only the "'resin of the wise'—a synonym for the transforming substance"—but also "the [alchemical} medium between mind and body and the union of both" (Jung, *Psychology and Alchemy* 161, 401). (In *Mysterium Coniunctionis* 481n91, Jung offers helpful root definitions of the word *spagyric:* either "to rend, tear, [or] stretch out" or "to bring or collect together.") *Magellan*

sparks in the pyre: i.e., soul-*sparks,* in Cabalistic texts, the spirit that descends into matter. *The Skin of the Rocket*

spars: "any pole, as a mast, yard, boom, or gaff, supporting or extending a sail of a ship" ("Spar" [n.], def. 1). *Matrix of Symbols*

spectrograph: here, "a versatile 'combi-instrument'"—both camera and *spectrograph*— that "spreads out the light gathered by a telescope so that it can be analysed to determine such properties of celestial objects as chemical composition and abundances, temperature, radial velocity, rotational velocity, and magnetic fields" ("Hubble's Instruments: STIS – Space Telescope Imaging Spectrograph" <https://esahubble.org/about/general/instruments/stis/>). *Restoring Hubble's Vision*

A spherical man responsive to birds: an allusion to the mystical androgyny of Christ, "the male paired with the female in Jesus's soul" (Jung, *Mysterium Coniunctionis* 373-74). In fact, even in the time frame of the most ancient cultures, "the primal hermaphrodite was frequently pictured as a sphere," a shape "that symbolized perfection and totality" (Chevalier and Gheerbrant, *The Penguin Dictionary of Symbols* 902). See also Christ's musing in Matt. 6.26: "Look at the birds of the air; they do not sow and reap and store in barns, yet your heavenly Father feeds them." *Erasure; Pioneer; Sphere*

spheroid: here, the Moon, an oblate *spheroid*. Although it is often assumed that the Earth, Moon, and Sun are spherical, "In reality, because of their rotational properties they are each slightly flattened into shapes known as oblate spheroids, the northern hemisphere [being] a little thinner than the southern [. . .]" (Duncan Steel, *Eclipse: The Celestial Phenomenon That Changed the Course of History* [Wash., DC: Joseph Henry, 2001] 51). *Copy; The Location of Earth*

spherules from the bin: any star perceived as a small sphere or globule embedded in the cosmic dustbin. *Link; Murphy's Law on Mars*

spire: here, "anything that tapers to a point, as a pointed structure capping a tower or steeple" ("Spire[2]" [n.], def. 3). *The Skin of the Rocket*

the Spot that we con: in Jupiter, the Great Red *Spot*, "which gushes up from below and is broken up to make red phosphorus as soon as it meets the sunlight" (Moore, *Travellers in Space and Time* 56). *Habitat*

Sprung from Jehovah, Adam in his prime: / Body, soul, and spirit: See Cor. 15.44-45: "If there is such a thing as an animal body, there is also a spiritual body. It is in this sense that Scripture says, 'The first man, Adam, became an animate being,' whereas the last Adam [Christ] has become a life-giving spirit." *Eternity's String*

Sprung from the dragon: In the *opus circulatorium*, the mercurial serpent is both "an image of the sun's course" and "the substance to be transformed" (Jung, *Psychology and Alchemy* 381-82). As Jung demonstrates, "Time and again the alchemists reiterate that the *opus* proceeds from the one and leads back to the one, that it is a sort of circle like a dragon biting its own tail [. . .]. For this reason the *opus* was often called *circulare* (circular) or else *rota* (the wheel) [. . .]." In other words, the hermaphroditic Mercurius, "the world-creating spirit concealed or imprisoned in matter," appears "at the beginning and end of the work: as dragon he devours himself and as dragon he dies, to rise again as the *lapis*" (293), the radiant stone, "a symbol uniting all opposites" (295). *Sphere*

Spun is the way that phenomena go: / The Archer on the hillside with His bow: Cf. Jung, *Psychology and Alchemy* 258, fig. 131—"Adam as *prima materia*, pierced by the arrow of Mercurius. The *arbor philosophica* [a symbol for the alchemical process] is growing out of him." Elsewhere Jung speaks of the identity of Mercurius with Christ (438), the second Adam, "a fascination that [has] never entirely disappeared" (431). However, in the Holy Sacrifice of the Mass, although "Christ the sacrificiant is also the sacrificed," the difference between the two is obvious and even palpable: "After the transubstantiation a piece of the host is mingled with the wine, thus producing the *coniunctio* of the soul with the body" and "establishing the living body of Christ, namely the unity of the Church" (310). *Exoplanets*

stables that we clean: in Greek mythology, Hercules' penitential cleansing of the Augean stables, both an act of supreme courage in the face of adversity and a symbol of the power of the human soul. See Chevalier and Gheerbrant, *The Penguin Dictionary of Symbols* 496. *Saturn's Pebble*

station: The International Space Station (ISS), a habitable artificial satellite launched into low-Earth orbit in 1998. *The Moon in Transition Raised to the Sun*

stave: here, either "a stick or [a] staff" ("Stave" [n.], def. 2) or even "a set of verses, or lines, of a song or poem; [a] stanza" ("Stave" [n.], def. 3). *Link*

the sternum: here, in the humanoid skeleton, the breastbone. *The Cutting Edge of Haptics*

the stinger: On 16 November 1984, in order to capture *Westar VI,* a rogue communications satellite, the astronaut Dale Gardner, flying a Manned Maneuvering Unit and riding *the stinger,* "a spear-like probe, [. . .] jetted over to the spinning satellite, [. . .] inserted the stinger and locked onto the motor nozzle. With bursts of his MMU jets, he stopped the satellite [from] spinning and then jetted back to the waiting orbiter. There, the RMS [the Remote Manipulator System] arm reached out and grasped a grapple pin on the stinger to capture the satellite. The satellite was then lowered into the payload bay. But the final stowing of the satellite had to be done by hand, proving once again the need for the human touch in space maneuvers" (Kerrod, *Space Walks* 50). *The Embodied Robot*

stone: in alchemy, the mysterious *lapis philosophorum,* the philosophers' *stone,* a symbolic "parallel of Christ" (Jung, *Alchemical Studies* 96, 320). See also 1 Pet. 2.5: "Come, and let yourselves be built, as living stones, into a spiritual temple; become a holy priesthood, to offer spiritual sacrifices acceptable to God through Jesus Christ." Not surprisingly, then, the alchemists themselves believed that "alabaster is whitest brain stone" and "is in every man" (Jung, *Mysterium Coniunctionis* 436n254). In fact, in the penultimate line of "Matrix of Symbols," even the speaker addresses his readers as "Alabaster hosts." *Centauri Dreams; Hyperspace; Matrix of Symbols; Moonwalker; Scion; The Shape of Things to Come; Skein Winder*

the stone is dry: The speaker refers to "the motif of torture"—a crucial element in "the phenomenology of the individuation process as the alchemists experienced it" and to one "gruesome" recipe in particular: "the drying of a man over a heated stone" (Jung, *Alchemical Studies* 328-29). Jung notes that, ironically, it is the artifex himself who, having projected himself into the material substance—the "stone"—of the opus, "cannot endure the torments" (329). *Clotho's Thrum*

A stone that is no stone: in alchemy, the philosophers' stone taken as a symbol of the united self, i.e., "of the inner Christ, of God in man" (Jung, *Alchemical Studies* 96, 291n9). *Matrix of Symbols; Ripples; Skein Winder*

The stone that is planted in man by God: the transformational *lapis,* both "the stone that has a spirit" and "the figure [of Christ] veiled in matter" (Jung *Alchemical Studies* 247). The note on *stone,* given above, is also relevant. *Centauri Dreams; Moonwalker; Skein Winder*

string: In *The Whole Shebang: A State-of-the-Universe(s) Report* (New York: Simon, 1997), Timothy Ferris indicates that, according to superstring theories, "Subatomic particles are tiny strings made of space. [. . .] Strings are so small that when viewed from a distance— meaning at any wavelength of light or any other form of electromagnetic illumination—they look like infinitesimal particles" (220). *Driven; Hyperspace*

strip: the Möbius *strip,* a possible universe in a higher-dimensional space; a continuous, one-sided geometric surface—i.e., a space warp "created by twisting a strip of paper 180 degrees and then gluing the ends together." In effect, "outside and inside are identical" (Kaku, *Hyperspace* 60-61). The "Möbius strip" is named after its deviser, the nineteenth-century German mathematician A. F. Möbius. *Hyperspace*

Stromatolite: "a laminated, sedimentary rock structure formed primarily in Precambrian shallow pools by mats of sticky, blue-green algae, which trapped layers of silt, esp[ecially] of calcium carbonate: [in fact,] these wavy or round formations serve as evidence for dating the first life forms on earth and are still being produced today" ("Stromatolite" [n.], def.]. *The Cradle of Life*

Subject to futility, species flee; / Accost the hill; incriminate the Tree: The speaker refers to Golgotha, the place of the skulls, and the Cross on which Jesus Christ was crucified. *Finger's Grain*

subset: here, Earth viewed as a data structure, a portion of a mathematical set. *A Map of the Runner's Route*

Subspace: in Mathematics, "a space which forms a proper subset of some larger space" ("Subspace" [n.], def.). *Hyperspace*

A subtile body: "a transfigured and resurrected body, i.e., a body that [is] at the same time spirit" (Jung, *Psychology and Alchemy* 427). Here, the word *subtile* is pronounced *SUB-till*. *Eternity's String*

such a flame as Spirals sleeve: The speaker refers not only to the gamma-ray glow of the Milky Way, but also to the stellar halo of Andromeda, its galactic twin, "two giant spirals on opposite ends of an even larger aggregation of about 20 galaxies called the Local Group" (Engelbrektson, *Stars, Planets, and Galaxies* 129). *Hyperspace*

Such clusters as glister: both galactic or open *clusters* and globular *clusters*. Sparsely populated, "Galactic clusters are found in the plane of the Milky Way. The *Pleiades* and *Hyades* in Taurus are well-known and familiar open clusters." By contrast, "Globular clusters are different in population as well as location in the Galaxy. These clusters contain stars that increase and decrease in brightness in less than a day. They are called RR Lyrae stars and are used to measure the distance of the clusters." In fact, "The stars of globular clusters, believed to be among the oldest in the Galaxy, are highly concentrated toward the center and number in the tens of thousands" (Engelbrektson, *Stars, Planets, and Galaxies* 116). *Driven*

Such crepuscules as swim: This phrase evokes the smooth, gliding motion of twilight after the sun has set. *The Cutting Ege of Haptics*

Sulfates: According to Alfred McEwen, a University of Arizona geologist, Melas Chasma [a canyon on Mars], despite "all its geologic riches, [. . .] lacks any obvious reservoir to keep a crew alive and provide fuel for their return rocket home." McEwen's solution is "to squeeze water from stones," moisture that must have "become locked into minerals in the rocks." In fact, "Images from HiRISE {NASA's High-Resolution Imaging Science Experiment] and other instruments suggest that Melas Chasma is rich in polyhydrated sulfates, minerals that by volume are up to half water." See Lee Billings, "No Man's Land: Where on Mars Should Astronauts Go?" *Scientific American* 4 March 2016: 11 <www.scientificamerican.com>. *Murphy's Law on Mars*

The Sun is my mentor: a pun—not only the star "rising in the east, crossing the sky by day, and setting in the west at dusk" (Engelbrektson, *Stars, Planets, and Galaxies* 13), but also Christ, the indwelling Son of God, "a wise, loyal adviser" ("Mentor" [n.], def. 1) who "surrounds [the speaker] even as a Muse" (l. 24), the poet's guiding spirit ("Muse" [n.], def.). *The Mill of the Host*

superposition: according to Paul Davies, "a hybrid of two overlapping realities [. . .]. But the inherent uncertainty of quantum mechanics forbids you to know which of these two possibilities will actually prevail" (*The Mind of God* 216). *The Quilted Multiverse*

superspace: the space of all geometries, i.e., a space of multiple dimensions supposed to contain actual spacetime and all possible spaces. *Hyperspace*

surplice (SIR-plis) *like a blouse:* "a loose, white, wide-sleeved outer ecclesiastical vestment for some services, ranging from hip length to knee length" ("Surplice" [n.], def.). *The Mill of the Host*

suture the twin: See the note on *He plants his boot; having sutured his seam*, a pertinent description of the "(physically) hyphenated astronaut" given above. *Finger's Grain; The Twin Paradox*

swain that yet trysts: the NASA astronaut, here conceived as Spacetime's "lover or suitor" ("Swain" [n.], def. 3) who arranges a meeting "at a specified time and place" ("Tryst" [vi.], def.). *Ripples*

synapse: "the minute space between a nerve cell and another nerve cell, a muscle cell, etc., through which nerve impulses are transmitted from one to the other" ("Synapse" [n.], def.). *The Inner Lives of Robots*

Synchronicity: "the simultaneous occurrence of a certain psychic state with one or more external events which appear as meaningful parallels to the momentary subjective state—and, in certain cases, vice versa" (Jung, *Synchronicity: An Acausal Connecting Principle* 25). The note on *I nudged a cloud once*, given above, is also relevant. *Copy*

a tangle of posts: the cross symbol—i.e., the crossbeam attached to the vertical beam, as in the crucifixion of Christ. See Jung, *Aion* 204. *Matrix of Symbols*

tantric: related to esoteric Hindu or Buddhist doctrines that emphasize interdependent ritual acts of body, speech, and mind. *In the Outposts of Space*

tau or tee: both "the primitive Egyptian form of the cross: T" (Jung, *Symbols of Transformation* 264n136) and, from the English alphabet, the letter T. In this poem, the word *tau* rhymes with "now." *Finger's Grain*

tectonics: "the study of the earth's crustal structure and the forces that produce changes in it" ("Tectonics" [n.], def. 2). *Habitat*

Teflon: the trademark for a white, waxy, synthetic cloth used in making the outer protective layer of an astronaut's spacesuit. *Self-Recollection*

The Teleoperator's Cue: See *YourDictionary* 2 June 2017: 1 <www.yourdictionary.com>: "One who operates (a robot, etc.) remotely" ("Teleoperator[2]" [n.], def.). See also "Teleoperation," *Revolvy* 1 <www.revolvy.com>: In research and technical communities, teleoperation refers to "operation at a distance." This is opposed to telepresence [. . .], a less standard term, which might refer to a whole range of existence or interaction" that includes "a remote connotation>." Accessed on 4 June 2017. *The Teleoperator's Cue*

Telepresent: The speaker refers to a sophisticated form of teleoperation—in effect, to an experience that resembles virtual reality. Thus, wearing a Helmeted Mounted [Stereo] Display (HMD), along with force and tactile feedback gloves, a human teleoperator senses—even as he simulates—the programmed actions of NASA's Robonaut. *The Teleoperator's Cue; The Twin Paradox*

Telluric, the ghost with the scythe: the Grim Reaper or Death, a telluric or earthly apparition often depicted as a skeleton wrapped in a shroud or a winding sheet and carrying "a tool with a long, single-edged blade set at an angle on a long, curved handle" ("Scythe" [n.], def.). *Self-Recollection*

template: "a pattern, usually in the form of a thin plate of metal, wood, plastic, etc., for forming an accurate copy of an object or shape" ("Template" [n.], def. 1). *The Location of Earth*

tesseract: a four-dimensional hypercube "that has been unraveled," or unfolded, as a series of "ordinary three-dimensional cubes [. . .] arranged in a three-dimensional cross"—in this poem, a symbol as well as a manifestation of our own "harrowing," unknown, "reassembled," and "seemingly impossible" universe. See Kaku, *Hyperspace* 70, 72-78, and also 72, fig. 3.7: Salvador Dali's 1954 oil-on-canvas painting *Crucifixion (Corpus Hypercubus)*, where the artist depicts Christ "as being crucified on a [crosslike] tesseract." *The Inner Lives of Robots*

Tharsis might vanish: In *Travellers in Space and Time*, Patrick Moore describes *Tharsis* as a ridge on Mars along which "a string of huge shield volcanoes spread out, the loftiest of them all [. . .] aptly called Olympus Mons or Mount Olympus," since "it towers to fifteen miles above the ground below." However, Moore still wonders whether Mount Olympus is either "extinct" or "merely dormant" (44-45). *Murphy's Law on Mars*

That Castor favored and that Pollux felt: See the note on *Castor* given above. *Moonplant*

Then meditate my days with Omphale: See the note on *Omphale's handmaid, Heaven's feigner* given above. *Skein Winder*

thermosphere: "the atmospheric zone or shell located above the mesopause [the site of the coldest temperatures in the atmosphere] beginning at an altitude of c. 85 km (53 mi.) and characterized by a great rise in temperature with increasing altitude" ("Thermosphere" [n.], def.). *Ripples*

Thinsulate: here, a synthetic thermal-insulation fiber used in the wayfinder's clothing. *Moonplant*

thrum: either "the row of warp thread ends left on a loom when the web is cut off" or "any of these ends" ("Thrum" [n.], defs. 1a and 1b). *Umbilicus*

till crescents date: here, at any time that less than half the waning (decreasing) Moon is lit by the Sun. *Gravity and the Robonaut*

Till some gas giant swirls or inside curls: here, an exoplanet the size of Jupiter, or even much larger, a hot disk "bound for a rebound." See the note on *Warm disks of dust rebound without a sound* given below. *Exoplanets*

Tinctures: The speaker refers to the divine tincture—a pneumatic essence—that, in this stanza, "Wholeness" extracts from the philosophers' stone, a Hermetic symbol of the unified self, i.e., "of the inner Christ, of God in man" (Jung, *Alchemical Studies* 96). See also 1 Peter 2.5: "Come, and let yourselves be built, as living stones, into a spiritual temple; become a holy priesthood, to offer spiritual sacrifices acceptable to God through Jesus Christ." *Self-Recollection*

Topology's fabric forever furled, / An umbilicus to some other world: In *Other Worlds*, discussing *Topology's fabric*: "the gross features and structure of space," Paul Davies suggests that "It is entirely possible that the universe on a large scale has a shape analogous to a torus, the world sheet curved over and rejoined with itself [. . .], a closed, finite but edgeless space" (97). However, later he adds that "Quantum mechanics implies that we must consider not one spacetime, but an infinity of them, with different shapes and topologies" (106). *Umbilicus*

torque of the chain: here, not only the rotational motor *torque* perfected by Robonaut 2, but also the force of "the infinitely luminous" Golden Chain that links Earth to Heaven (Chevalier and Gheerbrant, *The Penguin Dictionary of Symbols* 176). *Finger's Grain*

torus: the universe pictured as a hyperdoughnut, one of the "strange topologies" that Michio Kaku predicates in *Hyperspace* 94-98. *Hyperspace; The Shape of Things to Come*

To the top of the retort we ascend— / Become like a whirl; till the heating end, / Imprinted in the heart of matter tend / Time's imago mundi even as we blend: The speaker alludes to the "mystic logion" of Zosimos, a Gnostic alchemist: "And what meaneth this: 'the nature that conquers the natures,' and 'it is perfected and becometh like a whirl?'" Jung explains that, in alchemy, the "transforming substance is an analogy of the revolving universe, of the macrocosm, or a reflection of it imprinted in the heart of matter. Psychologically, it is a question of the revolving heavens being reflected in the unconscious, an *imago mundi* that was projected by the alchemist into his own *prima materia*" (Jung, *Psychology and Alchemy* 386), i.e., the stone that is a living thing: "the true hermaphroditic" Adam, who "bore his invisible Eve hidden in his body" (319n2). *Exoplanets*

trace: According to Jacques Derrida, the originator of deconstruction [a subversive theory of the practice of reading], "in any spoken or written utterance, the seeming meaning is the result only of a 'self-effacing' *trace*—self-effacing in that one is not aware of it—[a phenomenon] which consists of all the nonpresent differences from other elements in the language system that invest the utterance with its 'effect' of having a meaning in its own right. The consequence, in Derrida's view, is that we can never, in any instance of speech or writing, have a demonstrably fixed and decidable present meaning." See M. H. Abrams, *A Glossary of Literary Terms: Seventh Edition* (New York: Harcourt, 1999) 55, 57. *Link; Sphere*

Trismegistus' wand: the magic wand, or caduceus, of Hermes Trismegistus ("the Thrice-Greatest"), both the legendary first alchemist and emblematic magus. The staff bestows upon its wielder biological immortality. *The Cradle of Life*

turquoise: in Native American cultures, a sacred stone, with blue and green colors that signify the union of Heaven and Earth. *Matrix of Symbols; Magellan*

The turreted seahorse: According to Jennifer Kovac, "Seahorses have two [protuberant, turreted] eyes" that can move independently "in different directions. Their magnificent eyes allow the seahorse" not only "to find more food," but also to anticipate the movement of predators. See "Great Seahorse [*Hippocampus kelloggi*]," *BioWeb* <bioweb.uwlax.edu>). Last updated 15 April 2010. *Self-Recollection*

twice-born on the eighth: In the gospels of the New Testament, Christ is *twice-born* through His baptism in the Jordan. See also Jung, *Mysterium Coniunctionis* 399: "In the *Clementine Homilies* [2nd cent.] Adam is the first of a series of eight incarnations of the 'true prophet.' The last is Jesus." According to Jung, "The series consists of Adam, Enoch, Noah, Abraham, Isaac, Jacob, Moses, Christ" (399n107). Jung adds that "The eighth prophet is not merely the last in the series; he corresponds to the first and is at the same time the fulfilment of the seven, and signifies the entry into a new order" (401). The note on *infinite eight* given above is equally pertinent. *Cosmologist*

The Twin Paradox: in special relativity, a "bizarre phenomenon," as Paul Davies observes in *God and the New Physics*. Thus, "An itinerant twin blasts off to a nearby star, nudging the light barrier. The stay-at-home twin waits for him to return ten years later. When the rocket gets back, the Earth-bound twin finds [that] his brother has aged only one year to his ten." In other words, "High speed has enabled him to experience only one year of time, during which ten years have elapsed on Earth." Davies adds that "Einstein went on to generalize his theory to include the effects of gravity." In effect, "The resulting general theory of relativity incorporates gravity, not as a force, but [as] a distortion of spacetime geometry. In this theory, spacetime is not 'flat,' obeying the usual rules of school geometry, but curved or warped, giving rise to both spacewarps and timewarps" (121). *The Twin Paradox*

twins fraternal: in Greek mythology, Castor and Pollux, the offspring of Leda, both an Aetolian princess and, subsequently, a Spartan queen. However, Castor was the mortal son of Tyndareus, the king of Sparta, while Pollux was the divine son of Zeus. Nevertheless, when Castor died, Pollux shared his immortality with him. According to this version of the story, Zeus having pitied the brothers, "the two were never separated again." One day they dwelt on Earth, the next in Heaven, "always together" (Hamilton, *Mythology* 41-42). *Quest*

a two-slit screen: See the note on *Whether photons flit or particles hit, / As on a two-slit screen . . .* given below. *In the Outposts of Space*

Typhon: in ancient Greek lore, a "flaming monster with a hundred heads" and hissing viper coils (Hamilton, *Mythology* 67). *The Skin of the Rocket*

Umbilicus: the navel, or an umbilical cord. See the note on *Topology's Fabric forever furled, / An umbilicus to some other world* given above. *Umbilicus*

Unfolding the box, I peer through its slat; / Scan its contents; collusive as a cat, / Decouple its capsules; pursue its chat, / Till I ask the universe: What was that?: According to the probabilistic nature of the new physics, "the observer in the quantum-mechanical world" not only "manipulates," but also "participates" in every event that he perceives. He may even inhabit separate yet parallel realities. As Erich Harth demonstrates in *Windows on the Mind: Reflections on the Physical Basis of Consciousness* [New York: Morrow, 1982], "The situation has been described by a bizarre example known as 'Schrödinger's cat' [after the Austrian physicist Erwin Schrödinger (1887-1961)]. This hapless creature [the equally eerie counterpart of Alice's vanishing *Cheshire* cat] is locked in a box with a 'hellish contraption' consisting of a small amount of radioactive substance, a Geiger counter, a hammer rigged to be released by the counter, and a glass vial of cyanide placed to be broken by the hammer. The sequence of events is thus: particle from decay of radioactive substance triggers Geiger counter, Geiger counter trips hammer, hammer smashes vial, cyanide escapes and kills cat." However, "In the absence of an observation, the complete quantum-mechanical description of the radioactive substance would be that it has both decayed and not decayed, [with] the counter both tripped and not tripped, the hammer both up and down, the vial both smashed and intact, the cat both dead and alive." In short, given the Copenhagen or solipsistic view of quantum mechanics, "Only when [you] look is the matter decided one way or the other [. . .]." By contrast, given the many-worlds interpretation, "The moment you open the box to check on Schrödinger's cat, there will be two different worlds, one in which you observe a healthy cat jumping out of the box, the other in which *another you* finds the cat poisoned" (223-24). Incidentally, in the poem, *chat* is both a sign (in semiotics, the coded term for talk or chatter) and a homographic pun (the French word for cat, pronounced *shah*), a visual signifier that has two signifieds. *Copy*

Unfolds his unit: the Manned Maneuvering Unit (MMU), a jet backpack that enables an astronaut to fly independently of the shuttle orbiter. As Joels, Kennedy, and Larkin demonstrate in *The Space Shuttle Operator's Manual*, "The MMU is a self-contained backpack that latches onto your spacesuit. Two latches connect the MMU to your spacesuit's life-support backpack." Thus, "The latches allow you to don and doff the maneuvering unit by yourself" (3.14: 16). See also the note on *My unit manned* given above. *Hyperspace; Scion; The Shape of Things to Come; The Twin Paradox*

unravels his string: the human subject perceived as but a twisted thread, here disentangled from the cosmic coil. *Hyperspace*

Uracil: an RNA molecule involved in the transmission of genetic information. *The Cradle of Life*

uraeus: "the figure of the sacred asp or cobra on the headdress of ancient Egyptian rulers" ("Uraeus" [n.], def.). *Magellan*

Uranus: "the only green planet," yet with rings "as dark as soot" (Moore, *Travellers in Space and Time* 66). *Habitat*

Urim (YOOR-im) and Thummim (THUM-im): oracular gems used for casting lots and, here, set in Aaron's "breast-piece of judgement" (Exod. 28.30). *Moonwalker*

vas: See Jung, *Psychology and Alchemy* 236n15: The Hermetic vessel is "a circular instrument, a [well-sealed] phial of spherical shape." *The Quilted Multiverse; Restoring Hubble's Vision; Saturn's Pebble; The Skin of the Rocket*

Ventilates his limbs: See Joels, Kennedy, and Larkin, *The Space Shuttle Operator's Manual* 3.9: Beneath the Shuttle's spacesuit (the extravehicular mobility unit, or EMU), "you wear a cooling and ventilation garment similar to the ones worn by Apollo and Skylab astronauts. The garment is a one-piece affair made from Spandex mesh. Plastic tubing is woven into the mesh, and cool water from the life-support backpack circulates through the tubing to remove excess body heat. Air ducts attached to the garment provide ventilation to your limbs. This is a new feature; Apollo EMUs had ventilation tubes built into the space suits rather than the cooling garment." *Hyperspace*

vernal: "springlike; fresh, warm, and mild" ("Vernal" [adj.], def. 2). *Quest*

Vesta: NASA's *Dawn* spacecraft circled *Vesta*, both mammoth asteroid and intact protoplanet, in 2011. Apparently "Jupiter's immense gravity terminated its growth." See Marc Rayman, "The Giant Asteroid: A Retrospective," *Dawn Journal* 13 Jan. 2013: 2 <jpl.nasa.gov/blog/2013/1/the-giant-asteroid-a-retrospective>. *In the Outposts of Space*

Vitrify His plate: in the Holy Sacrifice of the Mass, the Paten, "A small plate of precious metal that holds the Sacred Host" (*Saint Joseph Sunday Missal* 10)—itself a Eucharistic vessel "finer than mere air" (Jung, *Alchemical Studies* 213). See the note on *Vitrify the* rebis given below. *Driven*

***Vitrify the* rebis:** to render pure, transparent, or clear, here referring to either "a breath-body or a subtle body not subject to corruption" (Jung, *Symbols of Transformation* 332), or the look-alike, transfigured, righteous coheirs of Christ (2 Cor. 3.18), or even "the consciousness-transcending fact [that] we call the self" (Jung, *Psychology and Alchemy* 202). *Wanderer*

Volcanoes erupt or else leak away: See Moore, *Travellers in Space and Time* 47: "There have been suggestions that the great Tharsis volcanoes erupt violently now and then, sending out enough gases (including water vapour) to thicken the atmosphere for a brief period; however, such conditions could not last, because the escape velocity of Mars is only 3.1 miles per second, and an Earth-type atmosphere would leak away." *Murphy's Law on Mars*

Vulcan's androids: See Peter James and Nick Thorpe, *Ancient Inventions* (New York: Ballantine, 1994), where the authors note that "The concept of robots, machines so skillfully crafted that they can perform the tasks of human beings and serve their creators' every wish, was no stranger to the ancient Greeks. It can be found in their earliest surviving poetry, composed by Homer in the eighth century B.C." Thus, "In his great epic the *Iliad* he describes some of the technological wonders produced by Hephaistos [Vulcan], god of metallurgy and craftsmanship," including "mechanical golden maid-servants, endowed with the gift of speech and intelligence. [. . .] Though fictional, Hephaistos' creations typify the ideals toward which some ancient Greek engineers aspired" (135-36). *Finger's Grain*

Wakened from the dead, I will walk with them: Cf. the promise of resurrection given by Jesus in John 14.18: "I will not leave you bereft; I am coming back to you." See also the alternate reading of this line—*I will dwell in them and thus walk in them*—given above. *Eternity's String*

Warm disks of dust rebound without a sound: The speaker refers to "a rebound mechanism by which giant planets that have moved close to their stars might then back out. In the new model [recently identified by Seth Jacobson, a planetary scientist at Michigan State University, and his collaborators], the planets 'rebounded,' moving in and then back out as the sun warmed up the gas in the disk and blew it off into oblivion. This rebound would have happened because, when a baby giant planet is bathed in a warm disk of gas, it feels an inward pull toward dense gas closer to the star and an outward pull from gas farther out. The inward pull is greater, so the baby planet gradually moves closer to its star. But after the gas begins to evaporate, a few million years after the star's birth, the balance changes. More gas remains on the far side of the planet relative to the star, so the planet is dragged back out." In fact, the rebound is a "shock to the system." See Rebecca Boyle, "How Are Planets Made? New Theories Are Taking Shape," *Quanta Magazine* 6 June 2022: 13-14 <http.://www.quantamagazine.org>. *Exoplanets*

water **is** *fire:* According to the alchemists, "the concepts of water, fire, and spirit coalesce as they do in religious usage." Thus, in the hymn of St. Romanus on the theophany [the direct, albeit temporary manifestation of God in sensible form], He "'who was seen of old in the midst of three children as dew in the fire, [was] now a fire flickering and shining in the Jordan, himself the light inaccessible'" (Jung, *Alchemical Studies* 74n31). *The Moon in Transition Raised to the Sun*

wave: in quantum physics, a probability *wave* that also functions as a particle. *Hyperspace*

We barrel down, onto its orbit latch, / Glimpse three elliptical moons that we match: The speaker pivots from Mars to Jupiter, where Juno, the NASA space probe, "will orbit the planet [. . .] with the hopes that it will collect data and images that offer clues to the origins of our solar system and the formation of the planets and moons." In 1995, twenty-one years earlier,

NASA's Galileo spacecraft "dropped a 750-pound probe into Jupiter's atmosphere [. . .] that confirmed ideas of how Jupiter's diaphanous rings formed out of dust particles blasted off Jupiter's small inner moons. It [also] measured the sizzling 2,800-degree temperatures of volcanoes on Io, one of the planet's four large moons, and it found evidence of under-ice oceans on the other three moons of Europa, Callisto, and Ganymede," each of which revolves around Jupiter in an *elliptical* orbit (Kenneth Chang, "What to Expect During Juno's Mission to Jupiter," *The New York Times* 4 July 2016: 1-2 <www.newyorktimes.com>). *Cosmologist*

We become a child and a fish at once: See Jung, *Symbols of Transformation* 198: "The fish in dreams occasionally signifies the unborn child, because the child before its birth lives in the water like a fish"; within weeks, during its fetal phase, "becomes child and fish at once"; and, like the astrological Christ, the first *fish* of the Pisces era, "is therefore a symbol of renewal and rebirth." *Rebis*

We cincture the cyborg: The speaker refers to the belted alb [the long white linen robe] of a priest's Mass vestments. In the Roman Catholic Church, the cord or cincture worn around the waist symbolizes the virtues of chastity and self-control. *Finger's Grain*

We fly by Jupiter: See the note on *We barrel down, onto its orbit latch, / Glimpse three elliptical moons that we match,* an overview of the *Jupiter* orbit given above. *Pioneer*

We ponder such waves as the cycles spent, / From aeon to aeon what the signals meant: Writing about "conformal cyclic cosmology," the mathematician Roger Penrose proposes that "the big bang was not actually the origin of our universe, but the continuation of the remote future of a previous aeon." In effect, "the universe cyclically balloons and compresses and what we refer to as the big bang is merely the beginning of this aeon, the period of the universe's life that we are [now] living through." In fact, Penrose maintains that we should look for "a signal coming from the previous aeon, which would suggest some consistency in the underlying physics between one aeon and the next" (Brooks, "Cosmic Thoughts" 36-37). *Cosmologist*

We pre-breathe in the airlock: On board a shuttle orbiter, the *airlock* is "an [air-tight] cylindrical chamber located at the end of the mid-deck," where astronauts don their spacesuits (Herrod, *Space Walks* 46) and then *pre-breathe* pure oxygen for a few hours in order to rid themselves of the nitrogen in their bodies that can cause gas bubbles and "bending" when they leave the orbiting station. *The Moon in Transition Raised to the Sun*

We reify the message in the ring: Here, the *ring* refers to elusive Time and indeterminate Space rendered real as a measurement of change. *Driven*

We siphon the symbol: See Jung, *Psychology and Alchemy* 238, fig. 121: "The transformations of Mercurius in the Hermetic vessel." Jung remarks that "One naturally thinks of this vessel as a sort of retort or flask; but one soon learns that this is an inadequate conception since the vessel is more a mystical idea, a true symbol like all the central ideas of alchemy." In fact, elsewhere Jung notes that "Transparent glass is something like solidified water or air, both of which are synonyms for spirit" (*Alchemical Studies* 197). *Wanderer*

We trail such terrain as stubble yet scars; / Lower the sky crane: NASA's Perseverance rover landed on Mars in 2021 "with the same sky crane maneuver [that] Curiosity used in 2012." During its landing, "A swooping robotic jetpack delivered Curiosity to its landing area and lowered it to the surface with nylon ropes, then cut the ropes and flew off to conduct a controlled crash landing safely out of range of the rover" (2). See Andrew Good, Karen Fox, and Alana Johnson, "Here's How Curiosity's Sky Crane Changed the Way NASA Explores Mars," *NASA Jet Propulsion Laboratory* <jpl.nasa.gov/news>. *Matrix of Symbols*

We witness Creation, headed toward Mars: Dennis Overbye suggests that "Mars has always been the backyard of our imaginations, the place [where] we might one day live or from where invaders would come in flying saucers to enslave us and steal our water. Our robots have already crossed that space again and again" ("Mars Is Frigid, Rusty and Haunted. We Can't Stop Looking at It," *The New York Times* 30 July 2018: 1 <www.nytimes.com>). See also Becky Oskin, "Why We're Obsessed with Mars," *Space.com* 5 Aug. 2012: 1-5 <www.space.com>. *Cosmologist*

where boulders are rife, / Curiosity still cuts like a knife: In order to investigate "Mars' habitability," NASA's Curiosity rover "drilled samples from 3.5 billion-year-old mudstone rocks in the 'Yellowknife Bay' formation of Gale Crater, the site of an ancient lake on Mars." Since mudstone was formed at Gale Crater when "very fine sediment [from volcanic rocks] settled on the bottom of a lake and was buried," organic carbon "was part of this material and got incorporated into the mudstone." Significantly, besides "liquid water and organic carbon, Gale Crater had other conditions conducive to life," including "chemical energy sources, low acidity, and other elements essential for biology, such as oxygen, nitrogen, and sulfur." In short, according to NASA's researchers, "this location would have offered a habitable environment for life, if ever it was present." See Bill Steigerwald, "NASA's Curiosity Takes Inventory of Key Life Ingredient on Mars," *NASA Jet Propulsion Laboratory* 27 June 2022: 3-4 <www.jpl.nasas-curiosity-takes-inventory-of-key-life-ingredient-on-mars> and also the note on "Curiosity steers" given above. Accessed 05-12-24. *Curiosity*

where sun-ships have flown: here, specifically, "NASA's Kepler planet-hunting spacecraft." See Overbye's note on *Kepler's super-Earth* given above. *Centauri Dreams*

Whether photons flit or particles hit, / As on a two-slit screen, Castor, admit— / Though millions of worlds yet sit, they are knit: an allusion to the double-slit (or two-slit) experiment conceived by the English physicist Thomas Young (1773-1829) that demonstrates not only the principle of wave-particle duality, but also the probabilistic nature of quantum matter. As Paul Davies explains in *Other Worlds,* "we know that any individual electron (being a tiny particle) can only pass through just one of the slits [as it travels from its source to a screen], so how does it know about the condition of the other one? In particular, how does it know whether the other is open or closed? It seems that the slit through which the electron does not pass (and which is, by atomic standards, an enormous distance away) has as much influence on the electron's subsequent behaviour as the one it actually passes through. [. . .] Phrased differently, the alternative worlds that could have existed, but did not come to do so, still influence the world that does exist, like the fading grin of the Cheshire cat in Alice's tale" (66-67). *Copy; In the Outposts of Space*

Who is this biped that wanders by day? / Some archaic species: click-speaker clay: According to Nicholas Wade, geneticists have found that "a previously unknown archaic species [. . .], a cousin of the Neanderthals, may have lingered in Africa until 25,000 years ago, coexisting with the modern humans and on occasion interbreeding with them." In fact, "Two of the hunter-gatherers in the study, the Hadza and Sandawe of Tanzania, speak click languages and carry DNA lineages that trace to the earliest branchings of the human family tree." See "Genetic Data and Fossil Evidence Tell Differing Tales of Human Origins," *The New York Times,* 26 July 2012: 27 <www.nytimes.com/2012/07/27/science>. *Wanderer*

wight: "a living being; [a] creature" ("Wight [1]" [n.], def. 1). *Wanderer*

Windmill: "either a mill operated by the wind's rotation of large, oblique sails or vanes radiating from a shaft" ("Windmill" [n.], def. 1), or "anything like a windmill, as a propeller-like toy," a *pinwheel,* "revolved by [the] wind" (def. 2). See also Jung, *Psychology and Alchemy* 307, fig. 158, "The Mill of the Host," where "The Word, in the form of scrolls, is poured into a mill by the four evangelists, to reappear as the infant Christ in the chalice." *Scion*

wind shear: "a sudden change in the direction of the wind, especially the dangerous vertical shifts encountered sometimes by aircraft near a runway" ("Wind Shear" [def.]). *Murphy's Law on Mars*

With a light-emitting diode display, / Checks his oxygen: "A chest-mounted microcomputer with a light-emitting diode [LED] display provides [the suited astronaut] with constant status checks of oxygen and battery power" (Joels, Kennedy, and Larkin, *The Space Shuttle Operator's Manual* 3.9). In effect, the semiconductor *diode* functions as a one-way switch for current. *Hyperspace*

With a percussive drill: i.e., "a drill on the end of the rover's robotic arm. This is used to grind clean (what geologists call 'fresh') spots for analysis, but it can also core out small cylindrical rock samples—hopefully to be retrieved and returned to Earth by a future mission" (Johnson, "Here's what the latest Mars rover has learned so far" 2). *Matrix of Symbols*

with both ridges and grooves: "The gyri [JYE-rye] and sulci [SUL-kye], or ridges and grooves located in the brain, are present [mainly] to increase surface area. This increased surface area is crucial for effective functioning [because] more neurons can be present in a brain with a flat surface." See Anthony A. Mercadante and Prasanna Tadi, "Neuroanatomy, Gray Matter," *NCBI Bookshelf* 24 July 2023: 1 <https://www.ncbi.nim.nih.gov/books>. *Murphy's Law on Mars*

With inch-worming arm and two-fingered hand, / [. . .] / Unhook attached components: details from NASA's view, now retrospective, of the piece-by-piece assembly of the 1-million pound International Space Station: Humankind "has begun a move off of the planet Earth of unprecedented scale. Astronauts will perform more spacewalks in the next [ten] years than have been conducted since space flight began, more than two and a half times as many. They will be assisted by an 'inch-worming' robotic arm; a two-fingered 'Canada hand'; and maybe even a free-flying robotic 'eye' that can circle and inspect the station" ("International

Space Station Assembly: A Construction Site in Orbit," *NASA Facts* June 1999: 1 <https://er.jsc.nasa.gov>). *The Moon in Transition Raised to the Sun*

without a seam: The speaker refers to the visible *seam* or portion of thread with which the opposites (e.g., light/darkness; consciousness/unconsciousness) are united, as in the symbol of the *rebis*. By contrast, in the higher Adam, "the opposition is invisible" (Jung, *Aion* 248). *Wanderer*

the world-egg cracked: See Chevalier and Gheerbrant, *The Penguin Dictionary of Symbols:* "The Psychic Egg, like the Cosmogonic Egg, contains both Heaven and Earth, the seeds of all good and evil, as well as the laws of rebirth and fulfillment of personality." However, here, like the foetus in the womb, the burgeoning coheir "feels shut in by his universe [. . .] and longs to escape by breaking the shell: he must accept the challenge in order to live" (340). *A Map of the Runner's Route*

The world is a Chariot: here, a dual mirror image of the alchemical *opus* and the hypothetical self. Thus, "one's given personality could be represented by a continuous circle, whereas the conscious personality would be a circle divided up in a definite way, and this generally turns out to be a quaternity. The quaternity of basic functions [thinking, feeling, sensing, and intuiting] meets this requirement. It is therefore only to be expected that the chariot should have four wheels to correspond with the four elements or natures." In other words, "The chariot as a spherical vessel and as consciousness rests on the four elements or basic functions, just as the floating island where Apollo was born, Delos, rested on the four supports which Poseidon made for it. The wheels, naturally, are on the outside of the chariot and are its motor organs, just as the functions of consciousness facilitate the relation of the psyche to its environment. [. . .] The 'chariot of Aristotle' [a recipe "Written of old and gathered by a certain Christian philosopher" in the "Tractatus Aristotelis ad Alexandrum Magnum"] can be understood in this sense as a symbol of the self" (Jung, *Mysterium Coniunctionis* 201-02n478, 203). *Exoplanets*

wormhole: in hyperspace, amid endlessly spawning universes, a crosscut from one place and time to another. *The Orphan in His Pram*

wraith: either "a ghost" or "the spectral figure of a person supposedly seen as a premonition just before that person's death" ("Wraith" [n.], defs. 1 and 2). *Cosmologist*

writing under erasure: According to Jacques Derrida—the originator and namer of deconstruction, a theory and practice of reading—"in any spoken or written utterance, the seeming [determinate] meaning is the result only of a 'self-effacing' trace." In short, "the differential play [. . .] of language may produce the 'effects' of decidable meanings in an utterance or text," but "these are merely effects" perpetually *sous rature* [*under erasure*] "and lack a ground that would justify certainty in interpretation" (Abrams, *A Glossary of Literary Terms* 57). *Erasure*

***xanthine* (XAN-theen):** a vital chemical compound found in most human body tissues. *The Cradle of Life*

yin and **yang:** in Chinese philosophy, the opposite feminine and masculine principles in the universe that acknowledge "the paradoxicality and polarity of all life" (Jung, *Alchemical Studies* 9). *Cosmologist*

yod: both the tenth letter of the Hebrew alphabet and the Gnostic symbol of the indivisible point, i.e., of the "perfect and indivisible man." Thus, "The Original Man, Adam, signifies the small hook at the top of the letter Yod [']" (Jung, *Aion* 218n136). The word rhymes with "wood." *Sphere*